FLAGS

• OF THE •

WORLD

FLAGS
•OF THE•
WORLD

NICOLE SMITH

CAXTON EDITIONS

Flags produced by Lovell Johns, Oxford, U.K. and authenticated by The Flag Research Center, Winchester, Mass. 01890, U.S.A.

All maps supplied by Malcolm Porter.

All Photographs supplied by Comstock Photo Library, London.

This Edition Published 2000 by Caxton Editions an Imprint of The Caxton Publishing Group

ISBN 1 84067 1203

Printed in Hong Kong.

Pages 2-3: The flags of many nations, proudly displayed.

These pages: The United Nations Headquarters in New York City, U.S.A.

The publisher would like to extend their thanks to Keith Lye F.R.G.S. in his capacity as consultant/editor.

Contents

Introduction

The foremost property of flags is that each one immediately identifies a particular nation, dependency or territory, without the need for explanation. The colours, shapes sizes and devices of each flag are often linked to the political evolution of a country embodying heraldic codes and often reflecting strongly held ideals, past and present philosophies and aspirations.

A flag can arouse patriotism and national pride, and a major insult may be felt if such a potent symbol is defiled.

We have become accustomed to the image of a new country achieving independence by means of a flag-hoisting ceremony. Very often, the new colours or arrangement will intend to signify goodwill, peace or democracy. In recent times, political upheavals in the former Yugoslavia, the former U.S.S.R. and other nations such as South Africa has led to a revision of boundaries, national identity and often the emergence of new nation states and hence new flags.

The Flag Institute has identified a number of areas of flag activity, all of which are continuing to grow. National flags may be used by governments or flown by private citizens. Flags may be designed for civil and military use. Other flags include those of semi-state institutions (such as national airlines), national institutions (such as the Royal National Lifeboat Institute), political organizations, voluntary and recreational organizations, commercial companies and corporations (with house flags and promotional flags of all kinds) and flags created for individuals. These areas of flag activity are all continuing to grow.

Flags are becoming increasingly important to all organizations throughout the world as powerful and evocative symbols of corporate as well as national identities.

This book is intended for the lay reader who will find it a valuable introduction to the fascination of vexillology (the study of flags). Each continent is dealt with separately to give the reader an appreciation of the overall geography of the region as well as the characteristics of each nation's flag. By examining

The World

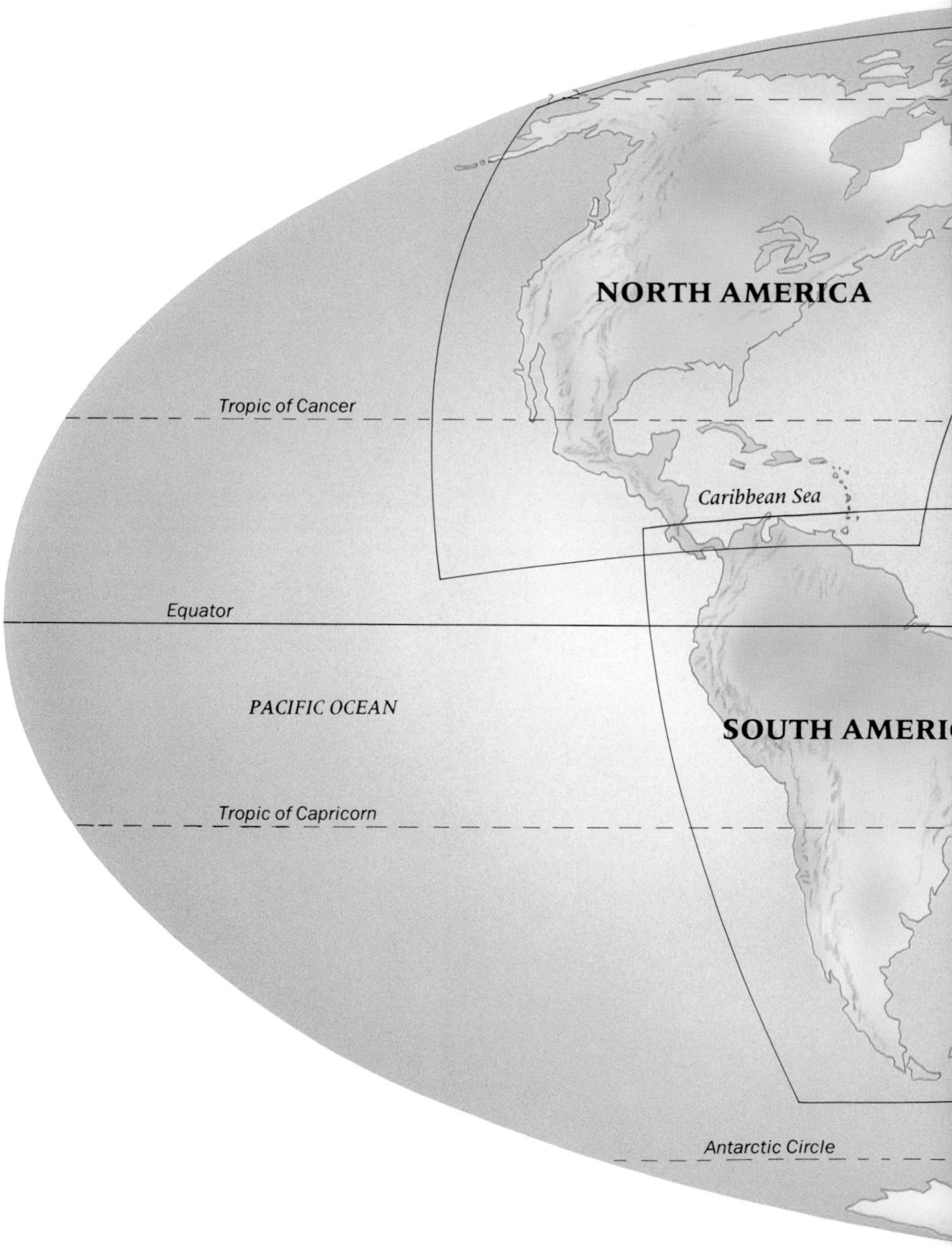

NORTH AMERICA

Tropic of Cancer

Caribbean Sea

Equator

PACIFIC OCEAN

SOUTH AMERIC

Tropic of Capricorn

Antarctic Circle

dependencies, territories, provinces and international organizations the reader gains a valuable insight into the evolution of the political world we live in today.

Details of population, capital cities, language and currencies provide a demographic and financial perspective though these aspects are forever changing and in some newly emerging countries it would be difficult to predict alterations in currencies or official languages. The information given here is based on the most up-to-date facts and figures available in May 1995.

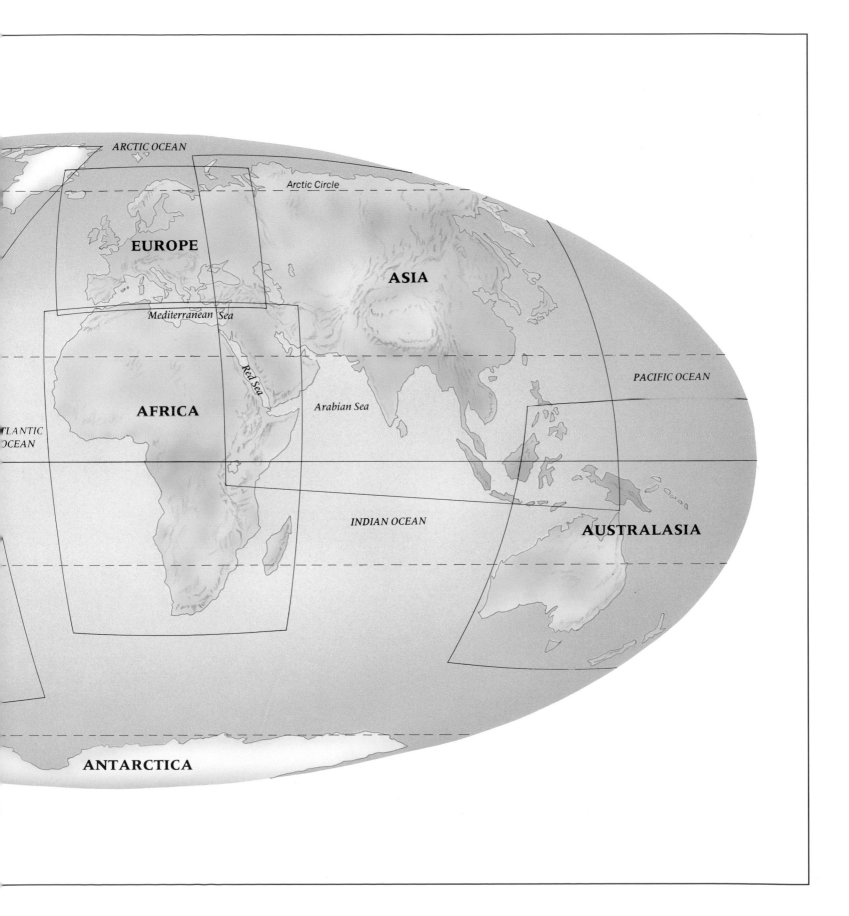

ARCTIC OCEAN

Arctic Circle

EUROPE

ASIA

Mediterranean Sea

Red Sea

PACIFIC OCEAN

AFRICA

Arabian Sea

ATLANTIC OCEAN

INDIAN OCEAN

AUSTRALASIA

ANTARCTICA

North America

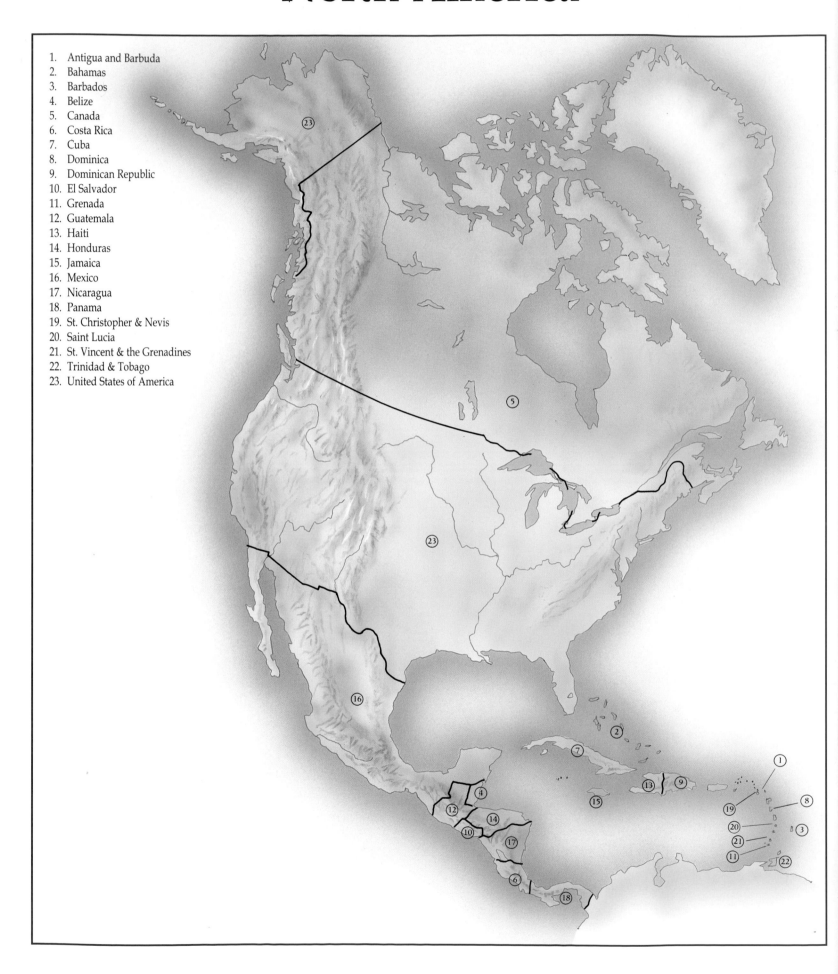

1. Antigua and Barbuda
2. Bahamas
3. Barbados
4. Belize
5. Canada
6. Costa Rica
7. Cuba
8. Dominica
9. Dominican Republic
10. El Salvador
11. Grenada
12. Guatemala
13. Haiti
14. Honduras
15. Jamaica
16. Mexico
17. Nicaragua
18. Panama
19. St. Christopher & Nevis
20. Saint Lucia
21. St. Vincent & the Grenadines
22. Trinidad & Tobago
23. United States of America

Antigua and Barbuda

Antigua and Barbuda are part of the Leeward Islands. The islands are dependent on tourism, cotton, sugar cane crops and lobster fishing. The flag was introduced, as a result of a competition in 1967 when the islands became self-governing. The red background stands for the dynamism of the people. The inverted triangle forms a victory V. The white and the blue stand for the sands and the seas. The yellow rising sun reflects the dawning of a new era and the sky reflects the African heritage. The flag remained unchanged when the country achieved independence in 1981.

Population: 67,000	**Capital:** *St. John's*
Languages: *English*	**Currency:** *East Caribbean dollar*

Bahamas

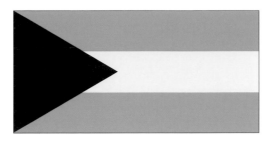

The Bahamas are made up of a coral-limestone archipelago of 700 islands and over 1,000 cays in the western Atlantic. The country's economy is largely dependent on tourism and the islands are characterized by golden beaches and aquamarine waters. The aquamarine and yellow stripes on the flag represent these two main features. The black triangle represents the unity of the nation and its inhabitants. This flag was introduced in 1973 when the country became independent.

Population: 266,000	**Capital:** *Nassau*
Languages: *English*	**Currency:** *Bahamian dollar of 100 cents*

Barbados

This densely populated island in the West Indies is made up of limestone and coral. The principal source of income of the island is tourism. It was a British colony from 1627 to 1966. The blue and yellow stripes represent the sea, the sky and the golden sands. Neptune's trident relates to the island's dependency on the sea. The shaft of the trident was removed to signify a break with the past and old traditions. The black stands for the African heritage. The flag was adopted in 1966 and was the result of a winning entry in a competition.

Population: 260,000	**Capital:** *Bridgetown*
Languages: *English*	**Currency:** *Barbados dollar*

Belize

Belize is an enclave situated on the coast of Central America. Formerly known as British Honduras, Belize gained its independence in 1981 having had a long struggle since 1950. This date is symbolized by the fifty laurel leaves surrounding the centre picture. For many years its main industry was logging. This is reflected in the centre of the flag which shows two timber workers with their tools. Beneath the shield is an inscription from the legend *Sub Umbra Floreo* (I flourish in the shadows). The thin red strips on the top and bottom of the flag symbolize the United Democratic Party.

Population: 205,000	**Capital:** *Belmopan*
Languages: *English*	**Currency:** *Belize dollar*

Canada

Canada is the world's second largest country divided into 10 provinces and two territories. Some 80 per cent of the land is uninhabited. The country was still technically under the British Imperial Parliament until 1931 when the creation of the British Commonwealth made the country a sovereign nation under the Crown. Prior to 1965, the British Red Ensign with the Canadian Arms was used but was unpopular with Canada's French population. The new flag we know today managed to break all affinities with both France and the U.K. and helped to unite the French and British with the indigenous population. The two red stripes either side represent the Pacific and Atlantic Oceans. These were originally meant to be blue but were changed to red, being an official colour of Canada. The red also represents the blood shed by Canadians who died in World War One. The white represents the vast snowy areas in the north of the country. The maple leaf is the traditional emblem of Canada.

Population: 27,815,000	**Capital:** *Ottawa*
Languages: *French, English*	**Currency:** *Canadian Dollar*

Costa Rica

Costa Rica lies in Central America with the Pacific Ocean on one side and the Atlantic on the other. Mountain ranges run through the whole length of the country. In 1824, Costa Rica gained independence and became a member of the Central American Federation along with Guatemala, Honduras, and Nicaragua. This flag derives from the CAF flag, but has been altered to include a red stripe through the centre.

Population: 3,267,000	**Capital:** *San José*
Languages: *Spanish*	**Currency:** *Colón of 100 centavos*

Cuba

Cuba is the largest island in the Caribbean. It has a varied landscape ranging from mountainous areas to fertile plains. Originally discovered by Christopher Colombus in 1492, the Spanish began to arrive from 1511. Cuba finally achieved independence in 1898 and developed a strong relationship with the U.S.A. In 1959, the right-wing dictator Fulgencio Batista was overthrown by Marxist revolutionary forces led by Fidel Castro. Cuba's new ally became the U.S.S.R. This flag was designed in 1849, but was not in use until 1901 when the Spanish finally withdrew from the island. The red triangle represents the blood shed during the struggle for independence.

Population: *10,896,000*	Capital:	*Havana*	
Languages: *Spanish*	Currency:	*Peso of 100 centavos*	

Dominica

Dominica is a mountainous island situated in the Caribbean and largely dependent on tourism. Dominica gained independence from Britain in 1978 after 11 years as a self-governing U.K. colony. The parrot on the flag is a sisserou, the national bird, only found on the island and was taken from a coat of arms. The stars represent the 10 island parishes. The red disc represents socialism, the green background, the country's vegetation and the cross Christianity. The three colours of the cross represent the Holy Trinity. The black stripe represents the African origins, the yellow the Carib people and, as ever, the white is for peace and purity.

Population: *72,000*	Capital:	*Roseau*
Languages: *English*	Currency:	*East Caribbean dollar*

Dominican Republic

Situated in the Caribbean, the Dominican Republic shares the island of Hispaniola, with Haiti occupying the western third. Once a Spanish colony, the country gained independence in 1821. Haiti then held the territory until 1844, when sovereignty was restored. The flag evolved during this period of Haitian rule. The flag's design stems from the Haitian flag but a white cross was added and the colours in the corners were rearranged.

Population: *7,447,000*	Capital:	*Santo Domingo*
Languages: *Spanish*	Currency:	*Peso of 100 centavos*

El Salvador

El Salvador is a small Central American country lying along the Pacific Ocean. Behind the coastal plain, where the majority of the population live, are high rugged mountains and volcanoes. Civil war since 1980 has wrecked the country, leaving the economy in tatters and many people homeless. However, a cease-fire took effect in 1992, but the country remains in a poor state. El Salvador gained independence from Spain in 1821, although the current flag only dates back to 1912. Blue and white flags are common to Central American countries who gained independence from Spain in 1821.

Population: *5,479,000*	Capital:	*San Salvador*
Languages: *Spanish*	Currency:	*El Salvador Colón*

Grenada

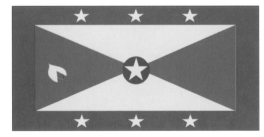

Situated in the Windward Islands, Grenada, nicknamed the Isle of Spice, also includes the Southern Grenadines. Grenada was a British colony from 1783 to 1974 when it became completely independent. Following a coup in 1979, the government was controlled by Marxist, Maurice Bishop. In 1983, Bishop was executed in a further coup and to put an end to the ensuing chaos, the U.S. sent in troops to restore democracy. Dating from independence in 1974, the seven stars on the flag symbolize Grenada's seven parishes. A major export is nutmeg, which is depicted within the triangle to the left of centre. Red stands for unity among the people, yellow for friendliness and sunshine, while green is for the island.

Population: *91,000*	Capital:	*St. George's*
Languages: *English*	Currency:	*East Caribbean dollar*

Guatemala

Guatemala is a highly populated country. It shares a mountainous terrain with both the Pacific and Caribbean coastlines. The country was first conquered by the Spanish in the 1520s. It remained under Spanish control until 1821 when independence was finally granted. The flag was adopted in 1871, but its origins date back to the Central American Federation (1823-1839), which was set up following the break from Spain in 1821. The CAF included Costa Rica, El Salvador, Honduras, Nicaragua and Guatemala. The blue and white stripes are common to many Central and South American countries. About half its people still speak the ancient Mayan language.

Population: *10,021,000*	Capital:	*Guatemala City*
Languages: *Spanish,*	Currency:	*Quetzal*

Haiti

Haiti, a mountainous country, is the second largest island nation in the Caribbean and takes up a third of Hispaniola. It was a French colony from 1697 to 1804 and remains French speaking. The country has been dogged by instability, coups and corruption. Multi-party elections were introduced in the 1990s, but in 1991 the military took over in the wake of the deposition of President Jean-Bertrand Aristide who was restored to office in 1994 with the help of U.S. troops. The flag adopted around the time of independence derives from the French tricolor although it has now developed into a horizontal arrangement of colours. The red band represents the mulatto community and the blue represents the black community. The official flag shows the country's arms on a white background with the motto 'Unity is strength' in the centre and a palm tree surrounded by weapons.

Population: 6,839,000	**Capital:**	*Port-au-Prince*
Languages: *French*	**Currency:**	*Gourde*

Honduras

Honduras is a mountainous country, like many others in Central America. The Spanish conquered Honduras in the 1520s and plundered the country for precious metals. However, in 1838, the country achieved independence. Mining remained important and is still an important part of the economy. Honduras was one of the five members of the Central American Federation consisting of Honduras, Guatemala, El Salvador, Nicaragua and Costa Rica. The flag officially adopted in 1949 derived from the CAF arrangements of the other members. The five stars symbolize the hope that the five nations of the CAF may eventually become a federation of states.

Population: 5,581,000	**Capital:**	*Tegucigalpa*
Languages: *Spanish*	**Currency:**	*Lempira*

Jamaica

Jamaica is one of the largest of the Caribbean islands. Much of the island is upland with tropical vegetation and high rainfall. The hated slavery trade was centred in Jamaica until it was dispersed in 1834. Independence from Britain arrived in 1962 when the flag was adopted. The gold colour represents the country's mineral wealth and sunshine, the green is for its agriculture and for hope and black for the hardships that the people have faced in the past through slavery.

Population: 2,415,000	**Capital:**	*Kingston*
Languages: *English*	**Currency:**	*Jamaican dollar*

Mexico

Mexico is the largest Spanish-speaking nation in the world and has a wide variety of physical features ranging from large areas of open basin-and-range country to areas of mountains and active volcanoes. The country became independent in 1821 and it was at this time that the green, white and red stripes were established, although the current flag was adopted in 1823. Mexico's arms, in the centre of the flag, are based on an Aztec legend and feature an eagle eating a snake while perched on top of a cactus on an island in a lake. This is the Aztec symbol for Mexico City.

Population: 86,712,000	**Capital:**	*Mexico City*
Languages: *Spanish*	**Currency:** *Peso*

Nicaragua

Nicaragua is one of the larger countries in Central America. It has a varied landscape, its mountain ranges broken up by fertile valleys and a large coastal plain. Until 1821, Nicaragua was part of the captaincy-general of Guatemala, which was ruled by Spain. In that year, Nicaragua declared independence, but this was short-lived as Nicaragua quickly became part of the Mexican Empire, but it broke away in 1823. It then became part of the United Provinces of Central America, but it left this union in 1838. The Nicaraguan flag, dating from 1908, is very similar to the flag of El Salvador, except for the shade of the blue and the motif in centre.

Population: 3,982,000	**Capital:**	*Managua*
Languages: *Spanish,*	**Currency:** *Córdoba*

Panama

With a hot, humid climate, Panama is a tiny country linking North and South America. Panama also links the Pacific and Atlantic Oceans with its canal. In 1903, Panama achieved its independence from Colombia, of which it had once been a province. Since independence Panama's government has changed many times. The flag dates back to 1903. Inspired by the Stars and Stripes, the blue stands for the Conservative Party, white for hope and peace and red for the Liberal Party. The red star stands for law and order and the blue star for civic virtues.

Population: 2,563,000	**Capital:**	*Panama City*
Languages: *Spanish*	**Currency:** *Balboa*

St. Christopher & Nevis

Situated in the Lesser Antilles, St Christopher (also known as St. Kitts) and Nevis are two islands. Originally colonized by Britain in 1713, the islands became independent in 1983 and this flag was adopted. The flag of the state was designed by a student as an entry in a competition. The colours represent green for fertility, yellow for sunshine, red for the struggle for independence and black for the African heritage. The two stars stand for hope and freedom. The colours of the flag are also associated with Rastafarians.

Population: *41,000*	**Capital:**	*Basseterre*
Languages: *English*	**Currency:**	*East Caribbean dollar*

Saint Lucia

Situated in the Caribbean, Saint Lucia was first settled by France in 1650 but it became British in 1814. It then changed hands between the two countries many times. Saint Lucia gained full independence from Britain in 1979. The flag dates back to 1967 when the country became internally self-governing and became an Associated State of Great Britain. The symbol in the centre of the flag represents the Pitons, twin conical volcanic plugs that rise impressively from the sea. The yellow represents the golden sands and the sunshine.

Population: *158,000*	**Capital:**	*Castries*
Languages: *English,*	**Currency:**	*East Caribbean dollar*

St. Vincent & the Grenadines

St. Vincent and the Grenadines are islands in the Lesser Antilles. The country became a British colony in 1783, self-governing in 1969 and finally independent in 1979. The flag is based on a design first used on independence and was the result of a winning entry in a competition. The three green diamonds, representing the islands as the 'gems of the Antilles', were added in 1985 replacing the island's coat of arms.

Population: *110,000*	**Capital:**	*Kingstown*
Languages: *English,*	**Currency:**	*East Caribbean dollar*

Trinidad and Tobago

Trinidad and Tobago are two islands off the coast of Venezuela, which have been linked politically since the late 19th century. First discovered by Christopher Columbus in 1498, the islands were settled by the French and the Spanish and then by the British. The state became independent in 1962 when the flag was adopted. Red is for the warmth of the sun and for the determination and courage of the people, black is for their strength and white represents the surf of the sea.

Population: *1,282,000*	**Capital:**	*Port-of-Spain*
Languages: *English,*	**Currency:**	*Trinidad and Tobago dollar*

United States

The United States of America is a federation of 50 states and is the world's fourth largest country. The U.S.A., being so large, has an enormous variety of landscapes and climates. In 1776, the U.S.A. declared independence from Britain and set up a federal republic. The flag was first adopted in 1777 during the War of Independence. The flag is known as the 'Stars and Stripes' and has become one of the most recognizable flags in the world. The stars on the blue canton represent the 50 states and the 13 red and white stripes represent the 13 original colonies who declared independence from the British.

Population: *258,063,000*	**Capital:**	*Washington D.C.*
Languages: *English*	**Currency:**	U.S. *dollar*

Ocho Rios - Jamaica

South America

1. Argentina
2. Bolivia
3. Brazil
4. Chile
5. Colombia
6. Ecuador
7. Guyana
8. Paraguay
9. Peru
10. Surinam
11. Uruguay
12. Venezuela

Dependency
13. French Guiana
14. Falkland Islands

Argentina

Known as the 'Land of Silver', Argentina is the world's eighth largest country and emerged as a nation state in 1816. With the Andes mountains to the west, much of central Argentina is covered by pampas grasslands. Patagonia covers the region to the far south. Argentina lays claim to the south Atlantic islands and part of Antarctica. Argentina unsuccessfully invaded the Falkland Islands (Islas Malvinas) in 1982. The blue and white triband was adopted by demonstrators following independence from the Spanish in 1810. The Sun of May was also adopted about the same time and it represents the sun that shone through the clouds on 25 May 1810 when the demonstrations first began in Buenos Aires. The flag was first hoisted by General Manuel Belgrano in 1812 when he was leading the revolution.

Population:	33,483,000	Capital:	Buenos Aires
Languages:	Spanish	Currency:	Argentinian peso

Bolivia

Bolivia, formerly Upper Peru, is today one of the poorest South American republics. It is a landlocked country which includes an area of the Andes and to the south-west covers part of the Amazon basin. Bolivia boasts Lake Titicaca, the highest navigable body of water in the world. Independence was established in 1825 from the Spanish who exploited its silver reserves. Bolivia was named at this time after its first president, El Liberador (The Liberator), Simon Bolívar. The flag has been the national emblem since 1888. The red stands for Bolivia's animals and the army's courage, the yellow for the metal resources and the green for the agricultural richness of the country.

Population: 7,064,000		Capital:	La Paz
Languages: Spanish,		Currency:	Boliviano
Quechua, Aymara			

Brazil

Brazil is a huge country covering nearly half of South America and is the 5th largest country in the world. It is a federation of 23 states and 4 territories including the Federal District. Brazil is home to the world's largest rain forest which is undergoing a rapid process of deforestation. Brazil declared itself independent from Portugal in 1822. In 1889, Brazil became a republic, but there were years of dictatorships and military rule before democracy returned in 1990. The sphere bears the motto Ordem e Progresso which means 'Order and Progress'. The states in Brazil are represented by the stars on the flag. The arrangement of stars is the night sky over Rio de Janeiro, the day the Emperor abdicated on 15 November 1889. Green represents the rain forests and the yellow diamond its mineral wealth.

Population:	156,406,000	Capital:	Brasília
Languages:	Portuguese	Currency:	Cruzeiro real

Chile

Chile occupies the south-west coast of South America, together with several South Pacific islands. It is the thinnest of the world's large countries forming a narrow strip along the western coast of the continent. Chile was a Spanish colony from the 16th century, but became independent on 1 January 1818. The design of the flag stems from this period and it is said to have been designed by an American called Charles Wood in the service of the freedom fighters. There is little doubt that the inspiration for this flag stems from the Stars and Stripes, white representing the snow-capped Andes, blue the sky and red the blood of those who sacrificed their lives for freedom.

Population:	13,813,000	Capital:	Santiago
Languages:	Spanish	Currency:	Chilean peso

Colombia

Christopher Columbus discovered what was to become known as Colombia in 1499. The Spanish conquest began some years later. Colombia emerged as an independent state from the Spanish Vice-Royalty of New Granada in 1819. The flag was adopted at this time. Colombia has suffered from instability with two civil wars. Its economy is based largely on crops, including coffee, bananas and cotton, although it has been said that the main contribution to the Colombian economy comes from drugs. The yellow represents the nation of Colombia, the blue, the sea and the severance of the domination of the Spanish. Finally, the red represents the loss of blood of the people during the fighting.

Population:	35,682,000	Capital:	Bogotá
Languages:	Spanish	Currency:	Colombian peso

Ecuador

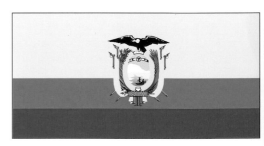

Straddling the Equator, it is from this geographical location that Ecuador took its name. Ecuador has a variety of landscapes, with high mountainous areas, an eastern alluvial area and a coastal plain. This flag is shared in different adaptations by Colombia and Venezuela. The colours were adopted by freedom fighter Francisco de Miranda in 1806. Independence was finally achieved from Spain in 1822, when Ecuador became part of Gran Colombia. Full independence came in 1830.

Population:	11,258,000	Capital:	Quito
Languages:	Spanish	Currency:	Sucre

Guyana

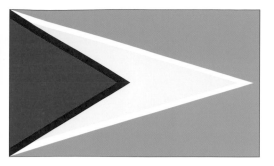

Guyana means 'land of many waters' and faces the Atlantic Ocean in north-eastern South America. The coastal area is below sea level with dykes to prevent flooding. Formerly known as British Guiana, Guyana gained independence from the U.K. in 1966 and adopted this flag. The red triangle represents the people's energy in building a new nation. The black border is for endurance and perseverance. The red arrowhead is for the country's mineral resources. The white is for the rivers and green is for the land.

Population:	812,000	Capital:	Georgetown
Languages:	English	Currency:	Guyana dollar

Paraguay

Paraguay is a landlocked country in South America. With a history of internal strife and conflict with its neighbours, Paraguay has had many setbacks. It was one of the first South American countries to gain independence from the Spanish in 1811. At this time, the tricolor flag was adopted, although it was not until a year later, in 1812, that the red, white, and blue colour scheme was established. The coat of arms was added in 1821 depicting the Star of May in honour of independence on 14 May. On the reverse side of the flag is shown the treasury seal – a lion and staff, with the words 'Peace and Justice'. This was added in 1842.

Population:	4,651,000	Capital:	Asunción
Languages:	Spanish, Guaraní	Currency:	Guaraní

Peru

Lying in western South America, Peru is made up of a narrow coastal plain, the mountain range of the Andes with part of the Amazon basin in the east. The Amerindians first arrived in Peru about 12,000 years ago. In the 16th century the country was conquered by the Spanish. Peru finally gained independence from Spain in 1824, but, since then, development has been slow with an unbalanced economy. Peru's flag dates from 1825. White represents peace and justice and red is for the people who lost their lives in the struggle for independence. The colour scheme dates from 1820 when the great liberation leader General José de San Martin claimed that a flock of red and white flamingo flew over his marching troops.

Population:	22,801,000	Capital:	Lima
Languages:	Spanish, Quechua	Currency:	New Sol

Surinam

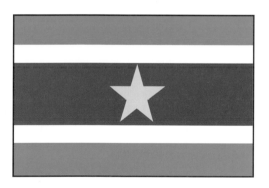

Surinam, formerly known as Dutch Guiana, lies between French Guiana and Guyana in the north-east of South America. The British were the first Europeans to colonize the country, but soon after, in 1667, the British handed over the territory to the Dutch. Surinam is a land of mixed races and religions. People of African, Asian and European descent make up the bulk of the population. Independence arrived in 1975 although the country still relies heavily on the Dutch for aid. The flag, adopted in 1975, features the colours of the main political parties. The star stands for unity of all the peoples and for altruism.

Population: 405,000	Capital:	Paramaribo
Languages: Dutch	Currency:	Surinam Guilder

Uruguay

Uruguay is officially known as the Eastern Republic of Uruguay. It is South America's second smallest independent state. It was the last Latin-American territory to secure its independence, in this case from Brazil. Independence came in 1828. Uruguay's flag dates from 1830. The nine blue and white stripes symbolize the nine provinces of Uruguay when it became independent. The colours of the flag and the Sun of May were taken from the Argentinian flag which represented the struggle against Spanish rule.

Population: 3,147,000	Capital:	Montevideo
Languages: Spanish	Currency:	Uruguayan peso

Venezuela

Venezuela (Little Venice) is situated in the north of South America. Venezuela was first discovered by Christopher Columbus in 1498 and later became part of the Spanish territory of New Granada. The country has a common history with Colombia and Ecuador and the three countries share similar flags. The yellow, blue and red were the colours of the Venezuelan freedom fighter, Francisco de Miranda. Blue is for the sea which divides Venezuela and its other dominions from Spain, which is represented by red and yellow. The seven stars represent the seven provinces of the Venezuelan Federation.

Population: 20,780,000	Capital:	Caracas
Languages: Spanish	Currency:	Bolívar

Rio de Janeiro, Brazil

1. Albania
2. Andorra
3. Austria
4. Belarus
5. Belgium
6. Bosnia & Herzegovina
7. Bulgaria
8. Croatia
9. Czech Republic
10. Denmark
11. Estonia
12. Finland
13. France
14. Germany
15. Greece
16. Hungary
17. Iceland
18. Ireland
19. Italy
20. Latvia
21. Liechtenstein
22. Lithuania
23. Luxembourg
24. Macedonia
25. Malta
26. Moldova
27. Monaco
28. Netherlands
29. Norway
30. Poland
31. Portugal
32. Romania
33. Russia
34. San Marino
35. Slovakia
36. Slovenia
37. Spain
38. Sweden
39. Switzerland
40. Ukraine
41. United Kingdom
42. Vatican City
43. Yugoslavia

Europe

Albania

Albania is a small country bordering the Adriatic Sea and has a mountainous interior. Albania was ruled by the Communists from 1944 until a non-communist government took over in 1992, but the years of isolation have left Albania the poorest country in Europe. Since 1912, Albania has used a flag with a double-headed black eagle. This was adopted by the national hero Iskander Bey (Skanderbeg), when Albania was part of the Ottoman empire. Skanderbeg drove the Turks from Albania in 1443. The red background to this flag symbolizes the blood shed in the nation's various struggles for independence.

Population	*3,421,000*	**Capital:**	*Tirana (Tiranë)*
Languages:	*Albanian*	**Currency:**	*Lek*

Andorra

A tiny, remote country placed high in the Pyrenees, Andorra's economy is mainly dependent on tourism and duty-free sales. Dating from 1866, the colours in the flag are said to reflect the principality's joint Franco-Spanish suzerainty, combining the red and blue of the French flag and the yellow of the Spanish. The flag also carries a coat of arms superimposed on the central yellow stripe bearing the motto 'United Strength is greater' reflecting the Franco-Spanish link. The mitre and crozier represent the Bishop of Urgel, the three red stripes on yellow, the Compte de Foix. An agreement between them in 1278 is responsible for the links with France and Spain. A democratic constitution was adopted in 1994.

Population: 63,000	Capital: Andorra la Vella
Languages: Catalan	Currency: French franc and Spanish peseta

Austria

Austria is mainly a country of mountains and forests with permanent snow and glaciers on the higher areas. Most of its population live in the east. Austria is a neutral country, pledged by law and treaties after World War II; but it joined the European Union in 1995. It was occupied by the Germans in 1938, and then by the allies in 1945, and the modern state did not regain full independence until 1955. The flag dates back to 1191 to the battle of Acre and during the Third Crusade when the only part of Duke Leopold V of Austria's tunic not bloodstained was under his swordbelt. The design was officially adopted in 1918 with the dissolution of the Austro-Hungarian Empire, although the colours had been in use since 1230.

Population: 7,937,000	Capital: Vienna
Languages: German	Currency: Schilling

Belarus
was Byelorussia

Belarus or 'White Russia' became independent from the U.S.S.R. on 19 September 1991. The country had been part of the Russian Empire since 1795, but officially became part of the U.S.S.R. in 1921. It is a low lying, landlocked country, with great forested areas. A Communist Republic within the Soviet Union, Belarus was one on the founding members of the Commonwealth of Independent States. The flag was first used in 1917 and was restored in 1991. The red and white come from a coat of arms.

Population: 10,319,000	Capital: Minsk
Languages: Belarussian, Russian	Currency: Rouble

Belgium

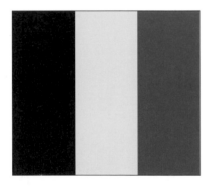

United as one of the 'Low Countries' after the Napoleonic Wars, Belgium has quite a varied terrain. The uplands of the Ardennes are to the south-east of the country comprising moorland, woodland and peat bogs. The lowland plains make up the rest of the country. Belgium is in a very significant part of Europe, being strategically placed in time of war and its central locality important in the European Union. The population is made up of Dutch and French speaking people with a small German minority. Each province has its own flag and the Belgian flag we know today derived from the arms of the provinces of Brabant, Flanders and Hainault. Although the flag is based on the French tricolor, it is interesting to note that the flag is almost square.

Population: 10,061,000	Capital: Brussels
Languages: Dutch, French, German	Currency: Belgian franc

Bosnia & Herzegovina

Since declaring independence in 1992, Bosnia-Herzegovina has been in a state of extreme chaos. It has a population dominated by Muslims with a slightly lesser number of Serbs and a minority of Croats. The Serbs within Bosnia, and from the other side of the border will not accept the Muslim-Croat alliance and the Muslim-dominated government is perpetually under attack. The future of this country remains uncertain. The flag was adopted with independence in 1992. The shield is a reference back to the ancient Bosnian monarchy. The lily is said to represent the *lilium Bosniacum*, a plant specific to Bosnia.

Population: 4,383,000	Capital: Sarajevo
Languages: Serbo-Croatian	Currency: Dinar

Bulgaria

Bulgaria is situated in south-eastern Europe, with its coastline on the Black Sea. Once ruled by the Turks as part of the Ottoman Empire, the country was liberated by Russian forces in 1878. Bulgaria stayed heavily dependent on Russia and later, after 1944, on the U.S.S.R. However, the Communist government fell in 1990. Since then, Bulgaria has been moving to a market economy. Today's flag was first adopted in 1878, after liberation. White represents peace, green stands for freedom and red for the blood shed by the freedom fighters. There can sometimes be an emblem on the flag which was introduced in 1947, but is now only used for official government occasions.

Population: 8,459,000	Capital: Sofia
Languages: Bulgarian	Currency: Lev

Croatia

Croatia has a long coastline along the Adriatic Sea. With the outbreak of war in 1991, Croatia has suffered some of the worst privations in what was once the former Yugoslavia. The War disrupted the economy, especially the tourist industry which was a major source of foreign exchange. Manufacturing for the export market was also affected. Croatia's flag dates back to 1848. The arms symbolize the various regions of the country.

Population: *4,788,000*		**Capital:** *Zagreb*	
Languages: *Croatian*		**Currency:** *Kuna*	

Czech Republic

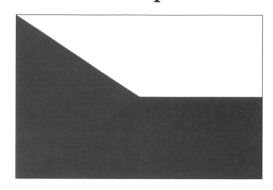

The Czech Republic, formerly part of Czechoslovakia, consists of two areas; Bohemia to the west and Moravia. In 1989 the Communist system was replaced with a multi-party democracy. This was a difficult transition and an upsurge of Slovak nationalism in 1992 resulted in the break up of Czechoslovakia, although ultimately the split was amicable. The split took place on 1 January 1993, the Czech Republic taking on the flag of the former Czechoslovakia. The red and white represent Bohemia, the blue triangle Moravia and Slovakia.

Population: *10,323,000*		**Capital:** *Prague*	
Languages: *Czech*		**Currency:** *Koruna*	

Denmark

The mainland part of Denmark is an extension of the North German Plain which is known as the Jutland Peninsula. Denmark also includes 406 islands of which 89 are inhabited. Denmark is one of the oldest monarchies in Europe and at one time had a large empire. The Faroe Islands and Greenland are still dependencies, but have a large degree of autonomy. The Danish flag is possibly one of the oldest flags in continuous use. It dates back to 1219, when King Waldemar II saw a vision of a white cross in the sky before the Battle of Lyndanisse. The red background represents the sullen evening sky of that night. The flag is known as the Dannebrog (the spirit of Denmark). The off-centre cross is common to all the flags of the Scandinavian countries.

Population: *5,191,000*		**Capital:** *Copenhagen*	
Languages: *Danish*		**Currency:** *Krone of 100 øre*	

Estonia

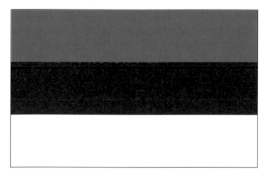

The smallest of the Baltic States, Estonia lies south of the Gulf of Finland with the Baltic Sea to the west. Once part of the Russian Empire, the Baltic States became part of the U.S.S.R. in 1940. Estonia and the other two Baltic States, Latvia and Lithuania, became independent in 1990. The flag was first used in 1918 and continued in use until 1940. It was re-adopted in 1988. The colour blue represents the sky, black is for the earth and white for the snows of Estonia's long winter.

Population: *1,546,000*		**Capital:** *Tallinn*	
Languages: *Estonian*		**Currency:** *Kroon*	

Finland

Finland is one of the most northerly states of mainland Europe. Part of the country lies on the Arctic Circle, and is known as the 'Land of the midnight sun', for in the summer, particularly in June, the sun shines all day and night. Finland has a history of Russian and Swedish influence, but became independent in 1917, after the collapse of the Russian Empire. It joined the European Union in 1995. The present flag was adopted soon after independence. The colours symbolize Finland's lakes (blue) and snow (white). The off-centre cross is typical of Scandinavian flags.

Population: *5,072,000*		**Capital:** *Helsinki*	
Languages: *Finnish, Swedish*		**Currency:** *Markka*	

France

After the Ukraine and Russia, France is the third largest country in Europe. It is composed of a wide variety of landscapes, including four different upland areas; the Alps, Pyrenees, the Massifs of Britanny and the Central Plateau. The large areas of lowland are drained by rivers such as the Garonne, Rhône, Loire and Seine. France has had a long history. The earliest conquerors were the Romans in 50 B.C. and the latest were the Germans who invaded in both world wars. The Germans are now one of France's closest allies. The flag dates back to the revolution of 1789 and is one of the most famous and recognizable flags in the world. The tricolor is said to represent liberty, equality, fraternity, the basis of the republican ideal.

Population: *57,650,00*		**Capital:** *Paris*	
Languages: *French*		**Currency:** *French franc*	

Germany

Germany stretches from the North and Baltic Seas in the north to the Alps in the south. The reunification of East and West Germany in 1990 has caused many problems, not least the huge cost of reconstruction. The new Germany not only retained the name, the Federal Republic of Germany, but also kept the original West German flag. The red, black and gold colours date from the days of the Holy Roman Empire.

Population: *80,769,000*	**Capital:**	*Bonn*
Languages: *German*	**Currency:**	*Deutsche Mark*

Greece

Greece has a mainland area extending into the Mediterranean Sea and around 2,000 islands, mainly in the Aegean Sea. Greece has been ruled by the Romans and the Turks over the centuries, but finally became independent in the early 19th century. At one time, the flag was a single blue cross, but this has since given way to the present flag. The cross represents Christianity and blue and white are the national colours of Greece. Blue is for the sea and sky and white for the purity of the freedom fighters who established Greece's independence.

Population: *10,376,000*	**Capital:**	*Athens*
Languages: *Greek*	**Currency:**	*Drachma*

Hungary

Hungary is situated in south-eastern Europe and consists of two lowland plains, encompassing some of the most fertile land in Europe. Hungary was defeated in World War I and at that time much of its territory was divided between Yugoslavia, Romania, and Czechoslovakia. In 1944, Hungary was occupied by the Red Army and a Communist State was established by 1949. Hungary became one of the many eastern European states dominated by the U.S.S.R. An uprising in 1956 against Soviet domination was brutally put down by Soviet troops, but this led the way for more progressive governments and a stronger degree of autonomy from the U.S.S.R. The colours of the Hungarian flag date back to the 15th century, but the flag was first adopted in 1919. The state emblem, first added in 1949, was removed in 1957.

Population: *10,280,000*	**Capital:**	*Budapest*
Languages: *Magyar*	**Currency:**	*Forint*

Iceland

Far out in the North Atlantic Ocean, Iceland is part of the mid-Atlantic ridge where the two great plates of North America and Europe meet. As a result, Iceland has many volcanoes, geysers and numerous other features relating to volcanic activity. Iceland has a long history of Scandinavian domination with Norway and Denmark both former rulers of the island. In 1944, Iceland became fully independent from Denmark following a referendum in which 97 per cent of the people voted for independence. The flag dates back to 1915 but became official on independence from Denmark. The off-centre cross, typical of the Scandinavian flags, dates back to a Danish legend and the colours are linked to other Scandinavian countries.

Population: *264,000*	**Capital:**	*Reykjavik*
Languages: *Icelandic*	**Currency:**	*Icelandic króna*

Ireland

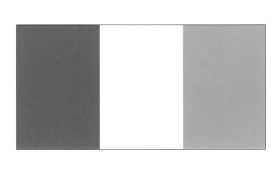

The Republic of Ireland occupies 80 per cent of the island of Ireland as the remaining 20 per cent is part of the United Kingdom of Great Britain and Northern Ireland. In 1921, Ireland became an independent state. It had been part of the United Kingdom for over 100 years. The flag dates back to 1848 and was used by freedom fighters in their struggle against the British. This came in the wake of the revolutions that were sweeping Europe in 1848 against post-Napoleonic conservatism. The flag was officially adopted after independence. The green represents the Roman Catholic Church, the orange the Protestants, with white representing the desire for peace.

Population: *3,569,000*	**Capital:**	*Dublin*
Languages: *Irish, English*	**Currency:**	*Punt*

Italy

Italy is dominated by two mountain ranges; the Alps and the Apennines which are separated by fertile plains. The islands of Sardinia and Sicily are also part of Italy. The north and south of Italy are very different in terms of culture and wealth, the north being much wealthier. Italy became a united country in 1861 when King Victor Emmanuel was proclaimed ruler. The flag dates back to Napoleonic times and was derived from the French tricolor, but the blue stripe being replaced by a green one. The green was inspired by the shirts of the Milan militia although it has been said that green was chosen by Napoleon as a personal preference when he invaded Italy in the late 18th century.

Population: *57,840,000*	**Capital:**	*Rome*
Languages: *Italian*	**Currency:**	*Lira*

Latvia

Latvia is a small state lying next to the Baltic Sea. Latvia has been a unitary state since 1991. Prior to independence, it had been part of the U.S.S.R. since 1944. As an independent country, Latvia maintains strong ties with the other two Baltic states, Estonia and Lithuania. The flag was adopted in 1991 but dates back to around 1280. One legend associates the flag with a Latvian hero wrapped in a blood-stained sheet. The white band symbolizes the justice, faith, trustworthiness and honour of the people of a free Latvia.

Population: 2,588,000	Capital: Riga
Languages: Latvian	Currency: Lats

Liechtenstein

The tiny principality of Liechtenstein is situated in the eastern Alps between Austria and Switzerland. The state consists of the two counties of Vaduz and Schellenberg. Liechtenstein shares its currency, customs and overseas representation with Switzerland but retains full sovereignty in other areas. The colours of the flag are traditional to the area, and was adopted in 1921. The yellow coronet was added to the flag in 1937. The flag can also be hung vertically with the crown rotated through 90 degrees.

Population: 30,000	Capital: Vaduz
Languages: German	Currency: Swiss franc

Lithuania

Lithuania is the largest Baltic state and like Estonia and Latvia, was annexed by the U.S.S.R. in the 1940s. Lithuania's annexation was regarded by a few Western governments, notably that of the U.S.A., as an illegal occupation. Lithuania was the first of the former Soviet republics to declare itself independent and non-Communist in 1990. The colours of the flag are said to symbolize Lithuania's forests and agricultural wealth. Red represents Lithuania's flora and the blood of her martyrs. The flag is also based on the predominant colours of the national costume.

Population: 3,747,000	Capital: Vilnius
Languages: Lithuanian	Currency: Litas

Luxembourg

Luxembourg is a tiny country located in central Europe and bordered by France, Belgium and Germany. It has been an independent state since 963 except for a period in the 1800s when Luxembourg shared the same king with the Netherlands. The colours of the flag date back to the Grand Duke's 14th-century coat of arms. The flag is very similar to the Dutch flag, except that the proportions are different and the Luxembourg flag has a paler blue.

Population: 397,000	Capital: Luxembourg
Languages: Letzeburgisch, French, German	Currency: Luxembourg franc

Macedonia

Once part of the former Yugoslavia, Macedonia became a unitary state in 1992. Although Macedonia is very close to the areas engaged in civil war, it has managed to avoid conflict. There is much tension between Greece and Macedonia over the name and flag of the country as the Greeks claim a historic right to the name going back to the time of the 'Greek Macedonian' Alexander the Great (356-232BC). The Greeks also claim that the 'Star of Vergina' is a 'Hellenic cultural possession'. In early 1993, The Untied Nations agreed to call the country the 'Former Yugoslav Republic of Macedonia'.

Population: 2,191,000	Capital: Skopje
Languages: Macedonian	Currency: Dinar

Malta

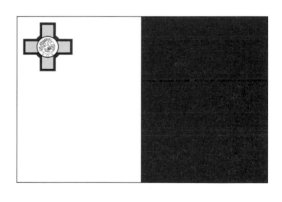

Malta is made up of three main islands and is situated in the middle of the Mediterranean Sea. Malta gained independence from Britain in 1964 and the flag was adopted at this time. The colours of the flag go back a long way to the time when Malta was the headquarters of the Knights of St. John of Jerusalem, who ruled the islands from 1530 to 1898. Their colours were red and white. The George Cross was added to the flag in 1943 to commemorate the bravery of the Maltese people during World War II.

Population: 362,000	Capital: Valletta
Languages: Maltese, English	Currency: Maltese lira

Moldova
previously Moldavia

Moldova is a densely populated country with many influences. The population is made up of 75 per cent Romanians, with the remaining 25 per cent Ukrainian and Russian. It became a unitary state in 1991 after the break up of the U.S.S.R. The flag was adopted in 1990 and is based on the Romanian flag. Moldova has expressed a wish to unite with Romania despite objections from Russia and the Ukraine. However in 1994, the people voted by a large majority not to join Romania. Instead, they decided to remain an independent country. According to official description the colours of the flag symbolize 'the past, the present and future' of Moldova.

Population: 4,356,000		Capital: *Chisinau*	
Languages: *Romanian*		Currency: *Leu*	

Monaco

Monaco is the second smallest independent state in the world. It is a principality ruled by the Grimaldi family since 1297. It comprises a rocky peninsula and a small stretch of coastline. Its income comes from banking, finance, tourism and its famous casino. The flag was established in 1881 and derives from the colours of the Grimaldi family's coat of arms which dates back to medieval times. The Monaco flag is the same as the Indonesian flag although the proportions are slightly different.

Population: 30,000		Capital: *Monaco*	
Languages: *French*		Currency: *French franc*	

Netherlands

The Netherlands is a low-lying country in northern Europe. It is a highly populated country, two fifths of which lies below sea level and is susceptible to flooding. Large areas have been reclaimed from the sea and for centuries inundation has been prevented by the construction of dykes and sand dunes along the coastline. The flag dates back to 1630 when it was first adopted and is one of the oldest flags in Europe. At the end of the 16th century, the Netherlands were part of the Spanish Empire. The fight for independence was led by Prince William of Orange of the House of Nassau-Dillenburg, who was assassinated by a Roman Catholic in 1584. The first flag was based on the livery of the Prince.

Population: 15,277,000		Capital: *Amsterdam*	
Languages: *Dutch*		Currency: *Guilder*	

Norway

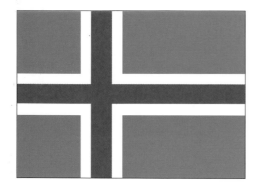

Situated on the Scandinavian Peninsula, Norway's sparse population is concentrated mainly in the southern part of the country. Norway's flag dates back to 1898 although it was used by merchants from 1821. The off-centre cross is typical of the flags of other Scandinavian countries and is based on a legend, which described King Waldemar II seeing a vision of a white cross in the sky before the Battle of Lyndanisse in 1219. The flag is essentially the same as the Danish flag but with the addition of the blue cross. The colour scheme represents Norwegian nationalism.

Population: 4,310,000		Capital: *Oslo*	
Languages: *Norwegian*		Currency: *Krone*	

Poland

Poland's position in Europe goes a long way to explain its complex and varied history. With constant invasions from neighbouring countries, it has been partitioned several times and re-founded twice this century. Poland was the first satellite country of the Soviet Union to bring down its Communist régime, which encouraged many other Eastern European countries to follow suit. The colours of the flag derive from the colours of the Polish coat of arms (a white eagle on a red field) which dates back to the 13th century. The flag, using red and white, was first used in 1919. Since 1989 when anti-communists took over, it has been a popular notion that the colours stand for peace (white) and socialism (red).

Population: 38,446,000		Capital: *Warsaw*	
Languages: *Polish*		Currency: *Zloty*	

Portugal

Portugal is situated on the Iberian peninsula on the Atlantic coastline. Important for its maritime and exploration history, it was the first European country to send a ship around the world. Portugal joined the European Union in 1986, but remains comparatively poor in relation to other European countries. The flag dates from 1910 when Portugal became a republic. Red symbolizes the revolution that took place and green is for hope and the sea. The central shield dates back to the 12th century. It was created when Alfonso I defeated five Moorish kings at the Battle of Ourique. The coat of arms is set on an armillary sphere, a nautical instrument which recalls the time of the Portuguese maritime voyages of exploration.

Population: 9,848,000		Capital: *Lisbon*	
Languages: *Portuguese*		Currency: *Escudo*	

Romania

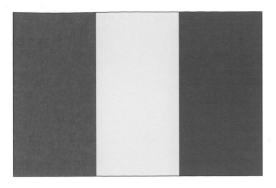

Dominated by the Carpathian Mountains and the lower plains of the Danube, Romania has a variety of landscapes. The two provinces of Moldavia and Wallachia united in 1861 to become Romania. The country became Communist in 1946. However, the Communist regime of Nicolae Ceausescu was defeated in 1989 and elections followed in 1992. Before the downfall of Communism in Romania, the flag bore the Communist arms in the central yellow stripe. The colours of the flag are those of Moldavia and Wallachia; the Wallachian colours being blue and yellow and the Moldavian colours blue and red.

Russia

The Russian Federation is a collection of republics and is the largest country in the world with a wide variety of landscapes and climates. The Communist system was established in 1917 when the Tsars were overthrown and the Russian Federation was part of the U.S.S.R. until 1991, when many of those republics broke away to form the Commonwealth of Independent States. The Russian Federation is the largest member. In December 1991 the national flag of the Soviet Union (hammer and sickle on red) was removed from the topmost tower of the Kremlin. The old Russian flag was then hoisted. The flag dates back to the 17th century as a mercantile flag of Russian vessels. These colours later became the 'pan-Slavic' colours.

San Marino

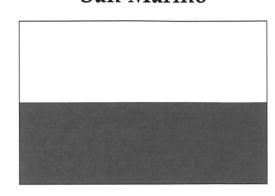

San Marino is one of the oldest states in Europe and is the world's smallest republic. The country lies completely within the territory of Italy and has been independent since A.D. 885. Tourism is the main activity, but there is some farming and manufacturing, mainly of craft goods. The flag is a simple bicolour symbolizing the snowy mountains and the blue sky. These colours derive from the country's coat of arms which dates back to 1787.

Population: 22,761,000	Capital: *Bucharest*
Languages: *Romanian*	Currency: *Leu*

Population: 148,537,000	Capital: *Moscow*
Languages: *Russian*	Currency: *Rouble*

Population: 24,000	Capital: *San Marino*
Languages: *Italian*	Currency: *Italian lira*

Slovakia

Slovakia was once part of the former Czechoslovakia, but in 1993, it amicably broke away and the two new states of the Czech Republic and the Slovakia continue to maintain close links with each other. The flag shows the pan-Slavic colours (see Russia above) with the state arms superimposed: a red background and a blue mountain with three peaks, with a white double cross on the centre. The flag dates from 1848, but was officially adopted in January 1993.

Slovenia

The country of Slovenia is situated in the northern part of the former Yugoslavia. Slovenia first became an independent state in 1991 when it seceded from Yugoslavia after a brief period of civil war which was less bloody than that suffered by Croatia. The flag shows the pan-Slavic colours of blue, white and red. The flag also shows the Slovenian state arms with a blue field and white mountain with three peaks representing the country's mountains and two blue wavy lines passing through its foot symbolizing the country's two main rivers, the Sava and Drava.

Spain

Spain is a large European country lying close to northern Africa. The country has varied landscapes with large areas of scrub, forests and mountains. Spain became united in 1579 when different independent kingdoms merged together. However, the colours of the flag date from the 12th century and were the colours of the old kingdom of Aragon. Today's flag dates back to 1938 and the time of the civil war. The 'excess width' of the yellow band is the result of a maritime requirement to make the Spanish flag more visible at sea.

Population: 5,345,000	Capital: *Bratislava*
Languages: *Slovak*	Currency: *Koruna*

Population: 1,993,000	Capital: *Ljubljana*
Languages: *Slovenian*	Currency: *Tolar*

Population: 39,125,000	Capital: *Madrid*
Languages: *Spanish*	Currency: *Peseta*

Sweden

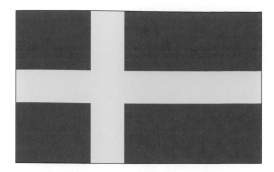

Lying on the eastern half of the Scandinavian peninsula, Sweden is a country of forests, fertile plains and lakes, much of which was shaped during the Ice Age. Sweden is one of the oldest Kingdoms in Europe. It joined the European Union in 1995. The colours of the flag are taken from an ancient state coat of arms dating from the 14th century, although there is evidence to suggest that the flag was used from 1449 onwards. The off-centre cross, common to all Scandinavian countries, derives from the Danish flag.

Population: *8,712,000*	**Capital:** *Stockholm*
Languages: *Swedish*	**Currency:** *Krona*

Switzerland

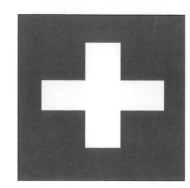

Switzerland is a mainly alpine country, with mountains covering 60 per cent of its area. Despite the four main languages of French, German, Italian and Romansch, Switzerland is a stable, united country enjoying high living standards. The Swiss flag dates from the 14th century and was used in the struggle for liberation from the Holy Roman Empire. Apart from the flag of the Vatican City, the Swiss flag is the only flag that is completely square. The reverse form of the Swiss flag became the flag of the Red Cross, founded in 1864, in honour of the Swiss philanthropist Henri Dunant.

Population: *6,977,000*	**Capital:** *Bern*
Languages: *German, French, Italian*	**Currency:** *Swiss franc*

Ukraine

The Ukraine is the largest country within the boundaries of Europe and is made up of fertile uplands with the Carpathian Mountains in the west. The north of the country is made up of lowlands. A great deal of the nation's agricultural land was ruined in the 1986 Chernobyl disaster when radioactive fall-out spread across the country. The Ukraine broke away from the former Soviet Union in 1991. The flag dates back to 1848 and the colours were used on a Ukrainian coat of arms. Originally used from 1918 to 1920, the flag was re-adopted in 1991.

Population: *42,141,000*	**Capital:** *Kiev*
Languages: *Ukrainian*	**Currency:** *Hryvna*

United Kingdom

The United Kingdom of Great Britain and Northern Ireland is made up of England, Scotland, Wales, Northern Ireland and many off-shore islands. The country is situated on the western-most edge of Europe and despite being situated in a northerly position, has a temperate climate due to the North Atlantic Drift. The flag dates from 1603 and combines the crosses of St. George of England and St. Andrew of Scotland. The Irish cross of St . Patrick, was added in 1801 to the flag as we know it today.

Population: *58,040,000*	**Capital:** *London*
Languages: *English*	**Currency:** *Pound sterling*

Vatican City

The Vatican City is the smallest independent state in the world. It lies within central Rome. It was created in 1929 to provide an independent base for the Roman Catholic Church. It takes its flag from the former civil ensign of the Papal States, dating from 1825.The emblem is the triple tiara of the Popes above the keys of heaven given to St. Peter.

Population: *1,800*	**Capital:** *-*
Languages: *Italian*	**Currency:** *Italian lira*

Yugoslavia
Serbia and Montenegro

Yugoslavia today contains the federal republics of Serbia and Montenegro. The name Yugoslavia dates from 1929 and means 'Land of the South Slavs'. The country has always had a turbulent history. In 1991, Slovenia and Croatia broke away and became independent with Bosnia-Herzegovina and Macedonia following in 1992. Further changes seem likely. The flag is based on the Imperial Russian Tricolor and what have become known as the pan-Slavic colours.

Population: *10,675,000*	**Capital:** *Belgrade*
Languages: *Serbo-Croatian*	**Currency:** *Dinar*

Asia

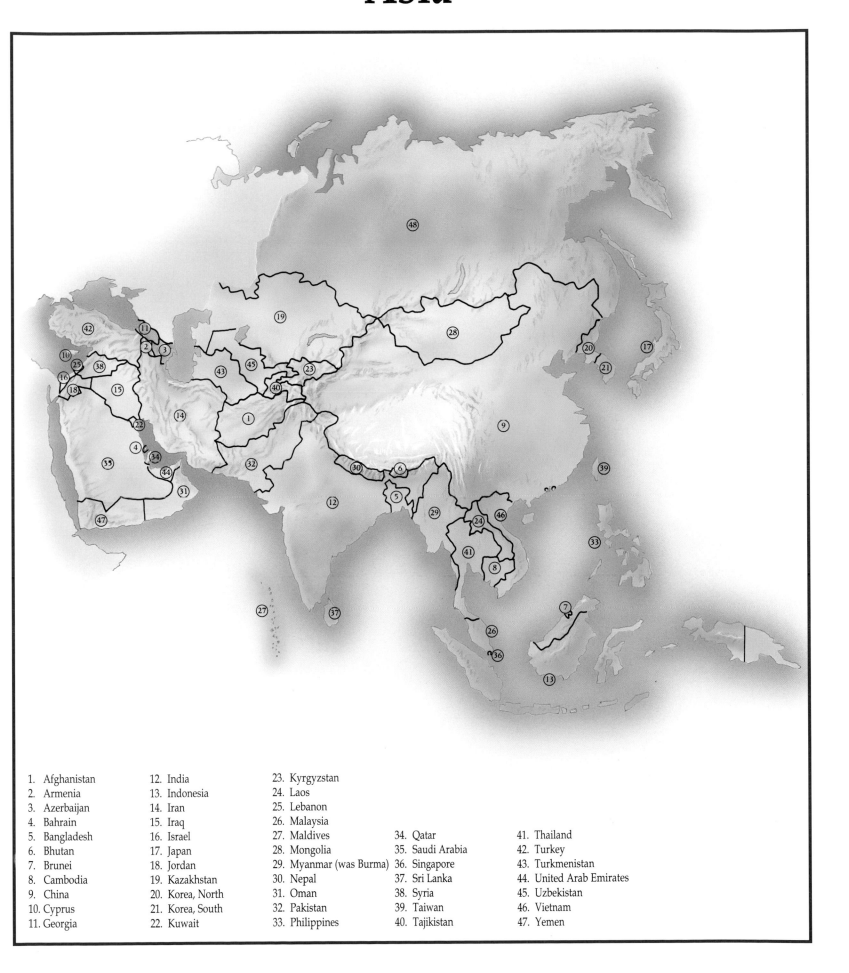

1. Afghanistan	12. India	23. Kyrgyzstan	
2. Armenia	13. Indonesia	24. Laos	
3. Azerbaijan	14. Iran	25. Lebanon	
4. Bahrain	15. Iraq	26. Malaysia	
5. Bangladesh	16. Israel	27. Maldives	34. Qatar	41. Thailand
6. Bhutan	17. Japan	28. Mongolia	35. Saudi Arabia	42. Turkey
7. Brunei	18. Jordan	29. Myanmar (was Burma)	36. Singapore	43. Turkmenistan
8. Cambodia	19. Kazakhstan	30. Nepal	37. Sri Lanka	44. United Arab Emirates
9. China	20. Korea, North	31. Oman	38. Syria	45. Uzbekistan
10. Cyprus	21. Korea, South	32. Pakistan	39. Taiwan	46. Vietnam
11. Georgia	22. Kuwait	33. Philippines	40. Tajikistan	47. Yemen

Afghanistan

A landlocked country, Afghanistan has had a turbulent history. The Khyber Pass being not only the gateway to India, but the back door to Russia, has caused numerous conflicts. The Soviet invasion of 1979-1988 and the following civil war lasting into the 1990s. The latest flag, adopted in 1992, uses colours employed by the Mujaheddin, the Muslim force which opposed Afghanistan's socialist government during the civil war. In the centre is the country's new coat of arms. Its main elements are the rising sun, the wheatsheaf, and the combined pulpit and prayer niche of the Islamic mosque.

Population: 22,143,000	Capital: *Kabul*
Languages: *Pashto*	Currency: *Afgháni*

Armenia

Armenia is a physically hostile, mountainous country, land-locked between unfriendly neighbours and still recovering from a recent earthquake. The economy is weak with little industry, although Armenia successfully produces tobacco and wine. In 1991, Armenia became independent from the U.S.S.R. although Armenia was first established in the 8th century B.C. as an independent kingdom. This flag, first used between 1812 and 1822, was re-adopted on 24th August 1990. Red represents the blood shed in the past, blue the land of Armenia, and orange the courage of the people.

Population 3,731,000	Capital: *Yerevan*
Languages *Armenian*	Currency: *Dram*

Azerbaijan

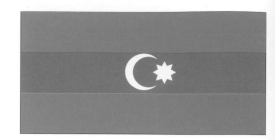

Azerbaijan is flanked by the Caspian Sea and the Caucasus mountains. It became independent in 1991, at the time of the breakdown of the U.S.S.R. Azerbaijan has an on-going conflict with Armenia over the predominantly Armenian enclave of Nagorno-Karabakh. There has been heavy fighting since the late 1980s. It is a land rich in natural resources with the potential to develop a successful economy in the future. Azerbaijan means 'Land of Flames', which comes from the fact that in many areas natural gas seeps up directly from the ground. The flag first came into being on 5 February 1991. The blue represents the sky, the red is for freedom and the green for the land and the Islamic religion. The crescent also represents Islam. There are eight ethnic groups in Azerbaijan and this is reflected in the eight points of the star.

Population: 7,435,000	Capital: *Baku*
Languages: *Azerbaijani*	Currency: Manat

Bahrain

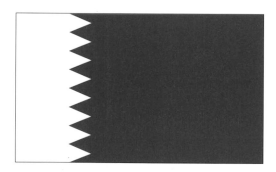

Situated off the coast of Saudi Arabia, 35 islands make up the country of Bahrain in the southern Gulf. Bahrain led the way in oil exportation which began in the 1930s. It is ruled by a hereditary Amir, and resumed its independent status in 1971. Its flag is based on the one used by several of the Gulf states, deriving from the flags of the Kharidjite sect of Islam. Originally, the flag was plain red with white borders added to signify acceptance of the General Treaty with the United Kingdom. The serration of the vertical stripe also came later in 1932 although the reason is not clear.

Population: 544,000	Capital: *Manama*
Languages: *Arabic*	Currency: *Bahrain dinar*

Bangladesh

Once described as 'golden Bengal', Bangladesh is mainly lowland and is home to the huge delta of the Ganges and Brahmaputra. This area frequently floods making life very difficult for its inhabitants. Once East Pakistan, Bangladesh was established in 1971. It is one of the world's poorest countries and has a rapidly growing and dense population which hinders economic growth. The green background is said to represent the fertility of the land as well as Islam and the red disc commemorates the blood shed in the struggle for freedom.

Population: 116,702,000	Capital: *Dhaka*
Languages: Bengali	Currency: *Taka*

Bhutan

Bhutan is a kingdom lying in the eastern Himalayas between India and Tibet. It is a remote, rural, country and dependent on agriculture producing mainly rice and maize. The wingless dragon grasping four jewels is Bhutan's national symbol. In the local language Bhutan is known as *Druk-Yul*, which means 'Land of the Thunder Dragon'. The two colours of the triangles have varied over the years, but the saffron yellow stands for the king's authority and the orange-red for Buddhist spiritual power.

Population: 1,532,000	Capital: *Thimphu*
Languages: *Dzongkha,*	Currency: *Ngultrum*

Brunei

Brunei is a tropical country made up of two enclaves bordering on Malaysia. Brunei was a British protectorate from 1888 to 1984. The Sultan of Brunei, reputed to be the richest man in the world, now rules by ancient hereditary rights. The yellow background to the flag represents royalty in the Malay world. The black and white stripes stand for the Sultan's two advisers, which denotes that he does not have total power. The arms were added in 1959. The inscription on the crescent is 'Always serve with the guidance of God'. The crescent itself symbolizes Islam. Under the crescent is a scroll bearing the legend 'Brunei, City of Peace'. The open hands are to indicate the goodwill of the government.

Population: *281,000*	Capital:	*Bandar Seri Begawan*
Languages: *Malay*	Currency:	*Brunei dollar*

Cambodia

With a tropical monsoon climate, three-quarters of Cambodia is forested. After French rule from 1863 to 1954, Cambodia finally achieved independence. The dictatorship of the Khmer Rouge and civil war has left Cambodia in an impoverished state. Following UN supervision, elections in 1993 introduced a government of national unity. Red is the traditional colour of Cambodia as well as being associated with Communism and revolution. The silhouette is the temple of Angkor Wat, the main temple dating from the 12th century and the blue symbolizing water, which is such an importance resource to the Cambodians.

Population: *9,633,000*	Capital:	*Phnom Penh*
Languages: *Khmer*	Currency:	*Riel*

China

China is a hugely populated country with 20 per cent of the world's people living here and is the world's third largest country. China became a republic in 1912. The following years were to be turbulent and there followed a long period of anarchy. Eventually, in 1949, the triumphant Communists declared a People's Republic of China in October and this is when the flag was introduced. The red and yellow are the traditional colours of China. Red is also the colour of Communism, with the larger star representing the guiding light of Communism. The smaller stars represent the four sections of Chinese society; the peasantry, the workers, the bourgeoisie and those capitalists who would participate in the ongoing revolution.

Population: *1,175,359,000*	Capital:	*Beijing*
Languages: *Chinese and variants, with local languages*	Currency:	*Yuan*

Cyprus

An island nation in the north-east Mediterranean, Cyprus is small but strategically placed. Since becoming independent from Britain in 1960, Cyprus has continued to witness the struggle between Turkish and Greek Cypriots and the island is still divided into two opposed states although the northern state is recognized solely by Turkey. The white background to the flag and the two olive branches are meant to signify peace and the map of the island represents a neutral portrayal of the country. Sadly, the flag seems to represents hope rather than reality.

Population: *726,000*	Capital:	*Nicosia*
Languages: *Greek, Turkish*	Currency: *Cyprus pound*	

Georgia

Georgia is positioned between Russia and Turkey. Land of the legendary Golden Fleece of Greek mythology, Georgia has a fascinating history and culture. It became part of the Russian Empire in 1800. In 1990 Georgia became independent following the Baltic States by leaving the former U.S.S.R. The flag was first used between 1917 and 1921 but was reinstated in 1990. The red-wine colour represents the good times, past and present. The black symbolizes the period of Russian rule and white the hope for peace.

Population: *5,456,000*	Capital:	*Tbilisi*
Languages: *Georgian*	Currency:	*Lary*

India

The subcontinent of India is the world's seventh largest country. Being so large, India has a wide variety of landscape and climates. Britain established a colony in the 1800s and its rule lasted until 1947 when India became independent. At this time India was subdivided into Hindu India and Muslim Pakistan. The non-violent freedom campaign was led by Mahatma Gandhi. The saffron colour represents the Hindus, the green the Muslims and the white is for peace. The wheel is an ancient symbol – the *Dharma Chakra*, or 'wheel of law'. The flag evolved during the struggle for independence.

Population: *900,543,000*	Capital:	New Delhi
Languages: *Hindi*	Currency:	Rupee

Indonesia

Indonesia consists of 13,700 islands, some of which are volcanic. Indonesia also extends into part of western New Guinea, which was acquired in 1963. The islands are mountainous and temperatures are high throughout the year. From the 1500s, the Dutch dominated the country and it was in 1949, after a four year struggle, that independence was achieved. The white band of the flag represents purity and the red stands for gallantry and freedom.

Population: *187,151,000*		**Capital:**	*Jakarta*
Languages: *Bahasa Indonesian*		**Currency:**	*Rupiah*

Iran

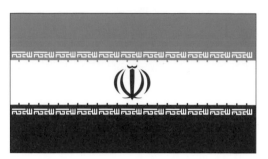

Before 1935, Iran was known as Persia. It borders the Caspian Sea in the north and has a varied landscape including mountains, deserts and high plateaus. Iran was ruled by its Shah until the monarchy was overthrown by the revolution in 1978 and the nation became an Islamic Republic under the Ayatollah Ruhollah Khomeini. The flag dates back to 1910 although the flag in its current form was adopted after the Shah was expelled. The emblem in the centre is a sword surrounded by crescents. This represents Islamic values and Allah (God). Along the edge of each stripe repeated 22 times are the words 'Allah Akbar' (God is great).

Population: *61,422,000*	**Capital:**	*Tehran*
Languages: *Persian*	**Currency:**	*Rial*

Iraq

The famous Tigris and Euphrates rivers make up the fertile crescent of Iraq. It was under strong British influence from 1916 and was ruled almost as a colony. The kingdom was ruled by the Hashemite dynasty until 1958 when it became a Republic. In 1968, control was taken by the Baathists. By 1979, Saddam Hussein had become president. The Iran-Iraq war of the 1980s devastated Iraq, but matters were made worse when Iraq invaded Kuwait in 1990. A multinational force drove Iraq back leaving the country in economic chaos. This is reinforced by harsh economic sanctions enforced by the international community. Iraq's flag dates from 1963 and includes all four pan-Arab colours. The three stars symbolize Iraq, Syria and Egypt. In the 1960s it was hoped that the three countries would eventually become a federation of states. However this is now very unlikely.

Population: *19,755,000*	**Capital:**	*Baghdad*
Languages: *Arabic*	**Currency:**	*Iraqi dinar*

Israel

The State of Israel was created in 1948 and marked the return of the Jews to their homeland. Israel is an arid country with half of its territory covered by desert. The people of Israel have worked very hard to reclaim swamplands and to irrigate the dry areas to make fertile farmland. The flag was designed in America in 1891 in the early days of the Zionist movement. The blue stripes represent the traditional colours of the Jewish prayer cloth. The star of David in the centre, is a centuries old symbol of the Jewish faith.

Population: *5,281,000*	**Capital:**	Jerusalem
Languages: *Hebrew, Arabic*	**Currency:**	Shekel

Japan

Situated off the Asian mainland, Japan is an archipelago of islands. The four main islands are Hokkaido, Honshu, Shikoku and Kyushu. These islands are situated in a geologically unstable zone where there are frequent volcanic eruptions and earthquakes. The recent earthquake in January 1995 killed over 5,000 people and injured many more. Japan is one of the oldest monarchies in the world and its Emperor is said to be the direct descendant of the Sun Goddess. The name Japan means 'The land of the rising sun' and this is represented in the flag. The redness of the disc denotes passion and sincerity and the whiteness represents honesty and purity.

Population: *124,845,000*	**Capital:**	Tokyo
Languages: *Japanese*	**Currency:**	Yen

Jordan

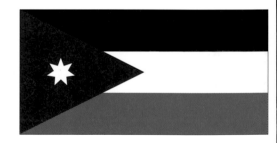

East of Israel, Jordan lies in an area of mostly desert with a small stretch of Red Sea coastline. After World War I, Jordan, then known as Transjordan was passed from Turkish to British control. The country became fully independent as Jordan in 1946. The flag is made up of the pan-Arab colours. The black, white and green represents the three tribes who led the Arab Revolt against the Turks in 1917, with red being the colour of the Hussein dynasty. The star represents the first seven verses of the Koran.

Population: *4,102,000*	**Capital:**	*Amman*
Languages: *Arabic*	**Currency:**	*Jordanian dinar*

Kazakhstan

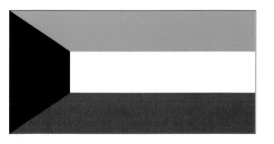

Kazakhstan is a very large country and mainly comprises vast steppes and desert. The climate is hot in summer and very cold in winter, typical of many continental countries. The country has been dominated by Russian régimes over the years, but in 1991 Kazakhstan led the break-away republics into the new Commonwealth of Independent States. Adopted in June 1992, the new flag has a blue background representing the skies and the golden sun and the soaring eagle symbolizes freedom. The vertical strip on the left of the flag is ornamentation.

Population: *17,169,000*   **Capital:** *Almaty (Alma-Ata)*
Languages: *Kazakh*   **Currency:** *Tenge*

Korea, North

Covering the northern part of the Korean Peninsula, the People's Democratic Republic of North Korea is largely mountainous and the climate can be harsh. After World War II, the country of Korea was split into two countries; North and South Korea. The north was influenced by the Soviet Union and a Stalinist government took over. The country is now very isolated and there is constant fear that war could break out with South Korea over territory. The flag shows traditional Korean design and colours, but also has the traditional red star indicating Communism.

Population: *23,051,000*   **Capital:** *Pyonyang*
Languages: *Korean*   **Currency:** *Won*

Korea, South

South Korea covers the southern area of the Korean Peninsula. It is a highly populated country and the landscape is mostly highland. After the partitioning of Korea, South Korea was established as a democracy. The economy grew rapidly and Korea became a significant exporter of manufactured goods. The flag was adopted in 1950. The central feature is the yin-yang symbol, which in Buddhism signifies nature's opposing forces. The white background is for peace and unity and the black symbols stand for the seasons, the points of the compass and the sun, moon, earth and sky.

Population: *44,065,000*   **Capital:** *Seoul*
Languages: *Korean*   **Currency:** *Won*

Kuwait

Kuwait is an emirate lying in the Arabian Gulf. Since 1756 it has been ruled by the al-Sabah family. It is largely desert and gets little rain. Kuwait was a British protectorate from 1914 to 1961 when it finally gained independence. It was occupied by Iraq in 1990 but a multinational force expelled the Iraqis in 1991. War damage, including the burning of oil wells, was extensive. The flag, dating from independence, features the four pan-Arab colours signifying unity.

Population: *1,461,000*   **Capital:** *Kuwait*
Languages: *Arabic*   **Currency:** *Dinar of 1000 fils*

Kyrgyzstan

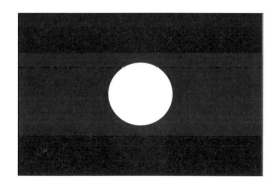

Kyrgyzstan is a remote, isolated, mountainous country in Central Asia. Independence was achieved at the time of the breakdown of the U.S.S.R. in 1991. There are disputes over its north-western border with China. The country has strong links with neighbouring Kazakhstan. The flag was first adopted in March 1992. The symbol in the centre is a yurt as seen from above. A radiant sun surrounds the symbol. The yurt, a house of skins lashed over a circular wooden frame, is the traditional symbol for the country's nomadic way of life. The rays of the sun represent the 40 tribes of Kyrgyzstan.

Population: *4,512,000*   **Capital:** *Bishkek*
Languages: *Kyrgyz*   **Currency:** *Som*

Laos

Laos is situated in south-east Asia. It is a landlocked, narrow country dependent on the Mekong River for transportation. Laos was once part of Indochina and ruled by the French. Independence was granted in 1954. Following independence came twenty years of bitter civil war. In 1975, the Communists took power. The country remains very poor. The flag was adopted by the Communists in 1975. The white disc is the the moon and signifies the well-being of the people, the blue stripe the Mekong River. The red either side of the river signifies the blood shed during the fight for independence.

Population: *4,511,000*   **Capital:** *Vientiane*
Languages: *Lao*   **Currency:** *Kip*

Lebanon

Bordering the Mediterranean Sea, Lebanon is a mountainous country. Lebanon has been influenced by French culture and, indeed, was ruled by the French from 1918 to 1944. After the country gained its independence, there was a period of thirty years of calm until civil war broke out in 1975. Muslims, Christians and Druses fought for control and the result is a war-torn land. The situation has been complicated by Israeli occupation of southern Lebanon. Officially, the civil war is over, but armed factions still control different areas of the country. The flag adopted on independence has the cedar tree in the centre. This has been the traditional symbol of Lebanon since biblical times.

Population:	3,855,000	Capital:	Beirut
Languages:	Arabic	Currency:	Lebanese pound

Malaysia

The present Federation of Malaysia comprises 13 states, partly in Malaya and partly in Borneo. The vegetation is rain forest in the lower areas, with montane vegetation on the higher ground. The official religion is Islam although there are many ethnic groups with many varying religions. This has caused tension in recent times. This version of the flag was first flown in 1963 although an earlier form dates back to 1950. The fourteen red and white stripes represent the 13 states and the federal territory of Kuala Lumpur. These stripes are said to date back to the 13th century. The crescent and star represent Islam. The blue represents Malaysia's British links and the yellow represents the states that are sultanates.

Population:	19,032,000	Capital:	Kuala Lumpur
Languages:	Bahasa Malay	Currency:	Malaysian dollar (Ringgit)

Maldives

The Maldives are an archipelago of around 2,000 islands and in fact Maldives means 'Thousand Islands'. The islands are scattered in a line in the Indian Ocean south-west of India. The islands were a British protectorate until 1965 when independence was established. The early flag of the Maldives was plain red, reflecting the culture of the numerous Arab traders who operated among the many islands. The later addition of the Islamic green panel and the crescent could also be attributed to the Arabian influence.

Population:	236,000	Capital:	Malé
Languages:	Divehi	Currency:	Rufiyaa

Mongolia

Sparsely populated with the arid Gobi Desert making up 25 per cent of the country with high mountains to the north and west, Mongolia is a large country which has been influenced by both the Soviet Union and China. Mongolia was one of the very first communist states, declaring itself as a people's republic as early a 1924. In 1946, Mongolia's independence was guaranteed by a treaty with the Soviet Union. The flag dates from 1940. Blue is the country's national colour. Red reflects the country's Communist past. The Golden Soyonbo is a Buddhist symbol, representing freedom. Within this, the flame symbolizes the promise of prosperity and progress.

Population:	2,372,000	Capital:	Ulan Bator
Languages:	Mongolian	Currency:	Tugrik

Myanmar (was Burma)

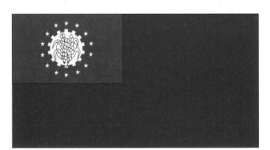

Until 1991, Myanmar was known as Burma. Adjacent to the Malay Peninsula, Myanmar is situated in a great structural depression. To the west are the mountains of the Arakan Yoma, and to the east rises the Shan Platea. 60 per cent of the country is forested. The people speak Burmese, a language related to Tibetan. The population also includes many minority hill peoples. Myanmar was annexed by Britain in 1895 and finally became independent in 1948 and left the Commonwealth. The present flag dates from 1948, but was revised in 1974. The flag of today shows 14 stars representing the country's states. The cog wheel represents industry and the rice-plant.

Population:	44,704,000	Capital:	Yangon (Rangoon)
Languages:	Burmese	Currency:	Kyat

Nepal

The Kingdom of Nepal is located in the heartland of the Himalayas and is the home of the famous Gurkha people who have dominated the country since the 16th century. The most striking feature of the Nepalese flag is its shape. This version of the flag dates from 1962 when the two triangular pennants were joined together. The crescent and moon represents the Ráná family who once held prime ministerial office and control of the nation and the sun symbol represents the country's royal family. Prior to 1962, both symbols carried human faces.

Population:	20,390,000	Capital:	Kathmandu
Languages:	Nepali	Currency:	Nepalese rupee

Oman

Oman is located on the south-eastern coast of the Persian Gulf. Since 1744, it has been ruled by the Sa'idi family, which also ruled at one time in Zanzibar and East Africa. The country has huge natural gas deposits and has been developing rapidly since the 1970s. The flag dates back to 1970 when it replaced the plain red flag typical of the Gulf states. However, the emblem is traditional and shows a dagger fastened over a pair of crossed sabres. Red is the nation's colour, the white symbolic of the traditional Imam of Oman and the green is for the mountain region of the country.

Population:	1,719,000	Capital:	Muscat
Languages:	Arabic	Currency:	Omani rial

Pakistan

Pakistan lies to the north-west of India and became separated from India in 1947. Created by the Muslim League, Pakistan is predominately a Muslim state. However, there are other religions in the country. East Pakistan (Bangladesh) broke way from the west in 1971 and Kashmir remains a disputed region between India and Pakistan. Civil war and the fear of Indian military intervention have seen Pakistan ruled by the military for much of its history. Democracy is now restored, led by Benazir Bhutto. The Muslim League created the flag and it dates back to 1906. The green flag with the white crescent and star are traditional to many islamic flags. The white stripe is to signify tolerance to Pakistan's other religions.

Population:	122,829,000	Capital:	Islamabad
Languages:	Urdu	Currency:	Pakistan rupee

Philippines

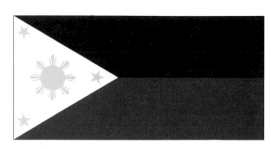

The Philippines is made up of over 7,000 islands. The two main islands Luzon and Mindanao take up much of the total area. The Philippines were ruled by the Spanish for 300 years until 1898 when the islands were ceded to the U.S.A. In 1986, the corrupt régime of President Marcos was overthrown and Cory Aquino was brought to office with Fidel V. Ramos becoming president in 1992.

The situation remains volatile. The flag was first used officially in 1946 when the country became independent from the U.S.A., although the flag was designed by nationalists in exile while the country was still controlled by Spain. Based on the stars and stripes, the eight rays of the sun stand for the island's provinces which declared independence from the Spanish. The three stars stand for the three main island groups, the white for purity and peace, the blue for idealism and the red for gallantry.

Population:	65,775,000	Capital:	Manila
Languages:	English, Filipino	Currency:	Philippine peso

Qatar

Qatar is situated on a barren peninsula in the Arabian Gulf adjacent to the United Arab Emirates. Much of its wealth comes from oil and gas, although it has recently started to diversify. Before 1820, many Arab countries had the plain red flags of the Kharidjite sect of Islam and this was how Qatar's flag originated. The maroon colour of the flag is said to derive from the effect of sunlight on a red flag. The white was added at the request of the British in 1820 to signify peace in the waters surrounding the country. The flag also has unusual proportions, being elongated in the proportion of 11:28.

Population:	520,000	Capital:	Doha
Languages:	Arabic	Currency:	Riyal

Saudi Arabia

Saudi Arabia is the largest country in the Middle East. However, the vast majority of the country is desert. The country has huge reserves of oil which produce great wealth. Dating from 1906, the flag is based on the country's Muslim religion. The inscription on the flag means 'There is no God but Allah, and Mohammed is the Prophet of Allah'. The sword stands for the Sa'udi family's determination to impose their rule on Arabia. The green background commemorates the Prophet Mohammed.

Population:	17,392,000	Capital:	Riyadh
Languages:	Arabic	Currency:	Saudi riyal

Singapore

Singapore is comprised of one main island with another 54 smaller islands situated off the south coast of the Malay peninsula. Singapore was a British colony from 1867 to 1959 when the country attained self-government. For two years between 1963 and 1965, Singapore became part of the Federation of Malaysia. In 1965, the country became fully independent. Adopted in 1959, the Singapore flag has the traditional Malaysian colours of red and white. The white is as ever for peace, virtue and purity and the red for the universal fellowship of mankind. The five stars stand for the five ideals on which the state is founded: peace, progress, justice, quality and democracy. The crescent represents the new and growing nation.

Population	2,867,000	Capital:	Singapore
Languages:	Chinese, English, Malay, Tamil	Currency:	Singapore dollar

Sri Lanka

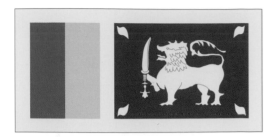

Sri Lanka lies south-east of India and until 1972 was known as Ceylon. The economy relies on tea, coconuts and rubber. Since independence, violence and civil war between the Sinhalese Buddhists and the Tamil Hindus has brought continuous strife to the country. The flag was adopted three years after independence from the British in 1948. The lion on the banner represents the ancient Buddhist kingdom and the stripes are for the country's religious and ethnic minorities, green for the Muslims and orange for the Hindus.

Population:	17,622,000	Capital:	Colombo
Languages:	Sinhala, Tamil	Currency:	Sri Lankan rupee

Syria

Syria lies on the Mediterranean Sea and stretches inland as far as the Tigris River with mountainous areas in the south and west. It lies at an important crossroads between Europe and Asia and this is reflected in its many historic and archeological sites. Syria officially became an independent country in 1946, but became part of the United Arab Republic, along with Egypt and Yemen, between 1958 and 1961. The flag dates back to 1958 and shows the colours of the pan-Arab movement.

Population:	13,394,000	Capital:	Damascus
Languages:	Arabic	Currency:	Syrian Pound

Taiwan

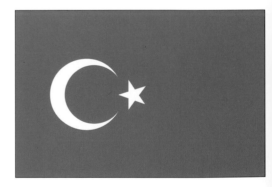

First colonized by the Chinese, Taiwan, formerly known as Isla Formosa, meaning 'beautiful island', was discovered by the Portuguese in 1590. However, in 1895, the province was seized by the Japanese. After World War II the country was returned to China, but became a refuge for Nationalists driven from China by Mao Zedong's forces. The red is for the nation of China and the rectangle shows a blue sky with a white sun representing the yang principle whose 12 points stand for the hours of each day and night.

Population:	20,926,000	Capital:	Taipei
Languages:	Mandarin (Northern Chinese)	Currency:	New Taiwan dollar

Tajikistan
(Tadzhikistan)

Tajikistan is mainly upland and lies between China, Kyrgyzstan, Uzbekistan and Afghanistan. Tajikistan became a unitary state in 1991 when it broke away from the U.S.S.R. Tajikistan is mainly an Islamic country and it remains very poor. The new flag dates from 1993 and shows a gold crown under seven stars. The colours of the flag derive from Tajikistan's previous flag when part of the U.S.S.R.

Population:	5,684,000	Capital:	Dushanbe
Languages:	Tajik	Currency:	Rouble

Thailand

Thailand (known as Siam until 1939) is a tropical country situated in South-East Asia. The country has been ruled by the Chakri dynasty since 1782. It is the only country in the region not to have been colonized by foreigners. During the 19th century, Thailand's flag featured a white elephant which was a traditional symbol of the country. However, this was removed in 1916 and in 1917 the central blue stripe was added as a gesture of solidarity with the Allies in World War I. The new colours of red, white, and blue were taken from the French flag.

Population:	58,824,000	Capital:	Bangkok
Languages:	Thai	Currency:	Baht

Turkey

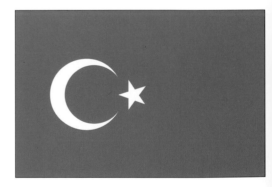

Turkey is a Muslim country, a small part of which is in Europe, while 97 per cent is in Asia. It was once the centre of the Eastern Roman (Byzantine) Empire and later the core of the great Ottoman empire which collapsed in World War I. Despite attempts to modernize, Turkey remains a lower-middle-income economy. The flag contains the crescent moon and five-pointed star – two symbols of Islam. These symbols, together with the red background, are also typical of the flags used by the Ottoman rulers.

Population:	59,461,000	Capital:	Ankara
Languages:	Turkish	Currency:	Turkish lira

Turkmenistan

Turkmenistan is extremely arid with the vast Kara Kum Desert covering 90 per cent of the country. In 1991, Turkmenistan broke away from the former Soviet Union and has since formed close relationships with Muslim countries to the south. The flag was adopted in 1992. Turkmenistan is an important producer of carpets, so the design is particularly appropriate. The five stars and the five elements of the carpet stand for the five main peoples in the country.

Population: *3,949,000* **Capital:** *Ashgabat (Ashkhabad)*
Languages: *Turkmen* **Currency:** *Manat*

United Arab Emirates

The U.A.E. is made up of 7 federated emirates and was formed in 1971. Abu Dhabi, Ajman, Dubai, Fujairah, Sharjah and Umm al-Qaiwain first amalgamated with Ras-al-Khaimah following in 1972. The U.A.E. lies on the Arabian Gulf and is hot and arid. The flag has all the pan-Arab colours signifying Arab unity and was formally adopted in 1971, although the flag dates back to 1916 when it was used in a revolt against the Turks.

Population: *1,723,000* **Capital:** *Abu Dhabi*
Languages: *Arabic* **Currency:** *U.A.E. dirham*

Uzbekistan

Uzbekistan lies between Afghanistan and Kyrgyzstan. The country declared its independence from the former Soviet Union in 1990 and became a member of the Commomwealth of Independent States in 1991. In 1991, the old Soviet-style flag was replaced by the current flag. The blue stands for Timur (Tamburlaine the Great) who once ruled Uzbekistan, white is for peace, green is for the country's natural vegetation and red is for vitality. The 12 stars represent the months of the Islamic calendar and the crescent moon is for the Islamic religion.

Population: *21,969,000* **Capital:** *Toshkent (Tashkent)*
Languages: *Uzbek* **Currency:** *Som*

Vietnam

Vietnam is situated in South-East Asia and is an amalgamation of the former states of North and South Vietnam. Once part of French Indo-China, Vietnam broke away from French control in 1954 which resulted in a Communist North Vietnam and a non-Communist South Vietnam. Despite American intervention, the whole of Vietnam became a Communist state in 1975. The flag dates from 1955, originally adopted by North Vietnam, but became the flag for the whole country in 1975. It uses the same red field as China with a single star symbolizing Communism.

Population: *70,881,000* **Capital:** *Hanoi*
Languages: *Vietnamese* **Currency:** *Dong*

Yemen

Yemen is located at the southern end of the Arabian peninsula. Since 1990, the Yemen Arab Republic (North Yemen) and the Yemen People's Democratic Republic (South Yemen) have been unified as the Republic of Yemen, though southerners fought unsuccessfully for secession in 1994. Dating from unification, the flag is composed of the pan-Arab colours signifying Arab unity.

Population: *13,463,000* **Capital:** *San'a*
Languages: *Arabic* **Currency:** *Yemeni dinar and Yemeni riyal*

One of Bangkok's beautiful temples

Hong Kong (New Territories)

Africa

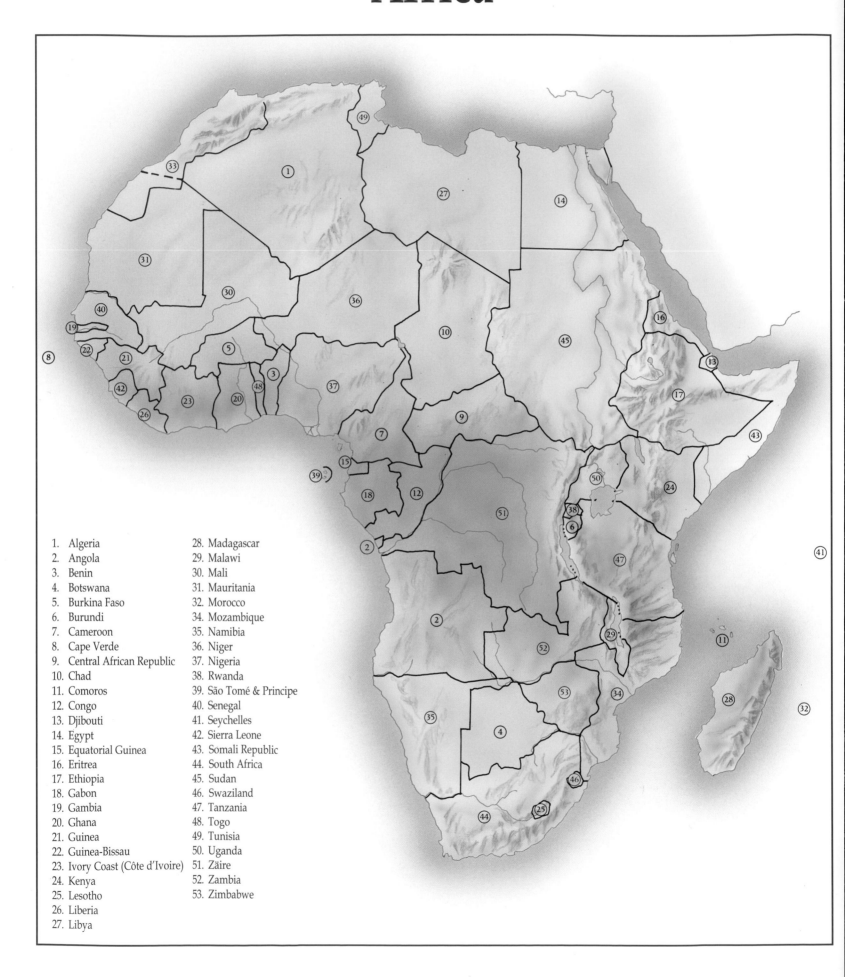

1. Algeria
2. Angola
3. Benin
4. Botswana
5. Burkina Faso
6. Burundi
7. Cameroon
8. Cape Verde
9. Central African Republic
10. Chad
11. Comoros
12. Congo
13. Djibouti
14. Egypt
15. Equatorial Guinea
16. Eritrea
17. Ethiopia
18. Gabon
19. Gambia
20. Ghana
21. Guinea
22. Guinea-Bissau
23. Ivory Coast (Côte d'Ivoire)
24. Kenya
25. Lesotho
26. Liberia
27. Libya
28. Madagascar
29. Malawi
30. Mali
31. Mauritania
32. Morocco
34. Mozambique
35. Namibia
36. Niger
37. Nigeria
38. Rwanda
39. São Tomé & Principe
40. Senegal
41. Seychelles
42. Sierra Leone
43. Somali Republic
44. South Africa
45. Sudan
46. Swaziland
47. Tanzania
48. Togo
49. Tunisia
50. Uganda
51. Zäire
52. Zambia
53. Zimbabwe

Algeria

Algeria is a large country, a great proportion of its area being covered by the Sahara Desert. The harsh climate has caused most of its population to congregate along the Mediterranean coast. After a bitter struggle between nationalist guerillas and the French, Algeria achieved independence in 1962 and has since been ruled by the *Front de Liberation Nationale*. The flag of this political party is now the national flag, but it originally dates back to the 1920s when it symbolized resistance to the French. As always, the green stripe symbolizes Islam, the white purity. The Islamic crescent and star are a universal badge of Islam. The red is symbolic of bloodshed.

Population: *26,882,000*	Capital:	*Algiers*	
Languages: *Arabic,*	Currency:	*Algerian dinar*	

Angola

Situated in south-west Africa, Angola has a widely varying climate and vegetation, from desert on the south coast to equatorial and montane conditions in the centre and north. After the arrival of the Portuguese in the late 15th century, it became a centre of the slave trade. Independence from Portugal was achieved in 1975. Potentially a wealthy country, Angola's development has been hampered by civil war. The five-pointed star, machete, and segment of a cog-wheel are clearly inspired by the hammer and sickle used by the former U.S.S.R., representing the industrial and agricultural workers. It is said that the yellow represents the country's rich natural resources and the red and black stripes have been used by other communist liberated nations to mean 'Freedom or Death'.

Population: *10,022,000*	Capital:	*Luanda*
Languages: *Portuguese*	Currency:	*Kwanza*

Benin

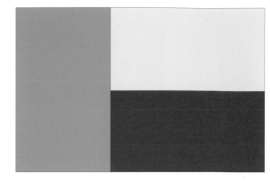

A small, equatorial country in West Africa, Benin has a hot, wet climate, with a rain forest belt. In the north, the country becomes savanna. Known as Dahomey until 1975, Benin has a history of Dutch, Portuguese and French colonial influence, and was much involved with the slave trade. Finally, the country gained independence in 1960, but it was not until 1991 that a multi-party democracy was established. The flag shows the red, yellow and green pan-African colours. Benin has another flag linked to its Communist history; a plain green flag with a red Communist star was used from 1975 until 1990 when Benin abandoned its socialist policies.

Population: *5,194,000*	Capital:	*Porto-Novo*
Languages: *French*	Currency:	*Franc C.F.A.*

Botswana

Situated in southern Africa, Botswana is made up of swampland, desert and scrubland. Botswana was formerly known as Bechuanaland and was a British protectorate until 1966 when it became independent. The white, black, white stripe is meant to symbolize racial harmony with Europeans and Africans living in peaceful coexistence. The blue colour represents water. A largely arid country, Botswana is dependent on a good yearly rainfall for its agriculture and its economy. The national motto is 'Let there be rain'.

Population: *1,402,000*	Capital:	*Gaborone*
Languages: *English,*	Currency:	*Pula*

Burkina Faso

Since independence from France in 1960, Burkina Faso, formerly Upper Volta has adopted a new name and a new flag. Situated in West Africa, it is a landlocked country and is mostly lowland. Burkina Faso means 'The Land of The Honest People' or 'The Republic of Upright Men'. The colours yellow, red and green, are the pan-African colours seen in many African flags signifying unity and fellowship with other ex-colonial African nations. The large yellow star symbolizes the revolution. The flag was adopted in 1984, when the country's name was changed.

Population: *9,830,000*	Capital:	*Ouagadougou*
Languages: *French*	Currency:	*Franc C.F.A.*

Burundi

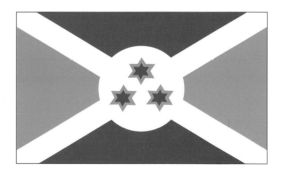

This small, landlocked, African country lies between Tanzania and Zaïre and supports a dense population. Burundi has a German and Belgian colonial history. It finally gained its independence in 1962 and a republic was established in 1966. It was in 1966 that the flag we know today was adopted. The three green-edged red stars stand for Burundi's motto 'Unity, Work, Progress' and also for the three ethnic groups of the country. Conflict between the two major groups, the Hutu and Tutsi, has marred the country's development. Green represents hope for the future, red the struggle for independence and white is the hope for peace.

Population: *5,974,000*	Capital:	*Bujumbura*
Languages: *Kirundi,*	Currency:	*Burundi franc*
French		

Cameroon

Cameroon is located in west-central Africa and its colonial history accounts for its French, British and German influences. It was ruled as a German protectorate until 1884, but ended up being divided between the French and the British. Independence was achieved in 1960-1961 when part of the British territory joined Nigeria. The federation of British and French states became a military state in 1972. However, a republic was created in 1984. The green, red and yellow are the pan-African colours. The design of the flag is based on the French tricolor, the yellow star representing liberty.

Population: 12,611,000	Capital: Yaoundé
Languages: French, English	Currency: Franc C.F.A.

Cape Verde

The Cape Verde islands lie off the coast of Senegal. They are volcanic and mountainous. The country belonged to Portugal from 1462-1974 finally becaming independent in 1975. The islands are poor and are poorly endowed with good natural resources and therefore dependent on foreign aid. This has led to a high rate of emigration. This is a very new flag, established in September 1992. The flag was adopted to signify the end of rule by PAIGC; 'Partido Africano da Independencia da Guine e Cabo Verde' and the movement towards democracy.

Population: 398,000	Capital: Praia
Languages: Portuguese	Currency: Cape Verde escudo

Central African Republic

Formerly known as Ubangi-Shari, the Central African Republic was once a province of French Equatorial Africa. Its rivers flow south into the Zäire basin and north to Lake Chad. Hence, it occupies a watershed area between the Zäire and Chad basins. It became independent in 1960. Since then, the Central African Republic has experienced difficulty, having one of Africa's most repressive régimes between 1966 and 1979. However, multi-party elections took place in 1993. The flag was adopted in 1958, two years prior to independence. The green, yellow and red signify pan-African unity. The red, white and blue represents the tricolor of the country's former ruler, France.

Population: 3,249,000	Capital: Bangui
Languages: French	Currency: Franc C.F.A.

Chad

A large state south of Libya, Chad is Africa's largest landlocked country and occupies part of the Sahara Desert. Chad achieved independence from France in 1960. It then suffered continuous civil war between ethnic groups in the north and south. The Aouzou Strip in northern Chad has also been occupied by Libya since 1973, but in 1994 the International Court of Justice ruled in favour of Chad. However, Libyan troops have remained there despite the ruling. The flag is a combination of the French tricolor, and the colours of pan-African unity. Blue represents the tropical sky, the streams and hope. Yellow represents the desert and the sun, and red represents the sacrifice for freedom and bloodshed.

Population: 6,131,000	Capital: N'djamena
Languages: French, Arabic	Currency: Franc C.F.A.

Comoros

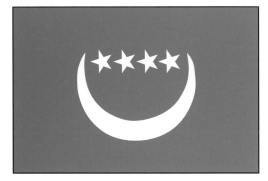

The Comoros Islands lie off the East African coast north-west of Madagascar. The islands became independent following a referendum in 1974 when ties were finally broken with France. However, the people of one island, Mayotte, voted to remain French. The islands make up one of the world's poorest countries. The crescent and the green background represent the Muslim faith and the four stars represent the four islands.

Population: 528,000	Capital: Moroni
Languages: Swahili, French	Currency: Franc C.F.A.

Congo

Congo is an equatorial country. The climate is extremely hot and there is rainfall all year round. Congo was part of French Equatorial Africa until it gained independence in 1960. It declared itself Communist in 1970 and remained so until 1990 when Marxism was abandoned. Elections were held in 1992 and a multi-party republic was created. The new flag was adopted in 1990 and bears the colours of pan-African unity.

Population: 2,508,000	Capital: Brazzaville
Languages: French,	Currency: Franc C.F.A.

Côte d' Ivoire

Lying in West Africa on the Gulf of Guinea, the Ivory Coast, since 1986, has been officially known by its French name as the Côte d'Ivoire. It has a tropical climate and substantial rain forests in the southern region. French influence dates back to the late-15th century when the trade in slaves and ivory became important. The country was controlled by the French from 1893 until 1960 when it became independent. The flag is a combination of the French tricolor and the pan-African colours signifying African unity. The orange stripe is for the northern savanna, the white for peace and unity and the green for the rain forests in the south.

Population: 13,358,000	**Capital:** *Yamoussoukro*		
Languages: *French*	**Currency:** *Franc C.F.A.*		

Djibouti

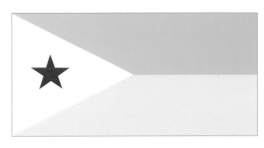

A small country in eastern Africa, Djibouti faces the Gulf of Aden and lies in a hot, arid unproductive plain. The country is strategically placed due to the railway link with Addis Ababa and is Ethiopia's main artery for overseas trade. Previously French territory, Djibouti gained independence in 1977 and it was at this time that the flag was adopted. The two main ethnic groups are the Afars and the Issas. The green is for the Afars and the blue for the Issas. The white is for peace and the red, five-pointed star is for unity and independence.

Population: 574,000	**Capital:** *Djibouti*
Languages: *Arabic, French*	**Currency:** *Djibouti franc*

Egypt

Egypt is a large country with a third of its area being taken up by desert. The fertile Nile Valley and its delta support 96 per cent of the population. Egypt was part of the Ottoman Empire from 1517, although British influence became important later. The country was a British protectorate from 1914 to 1922 when it became partially independent. The present republic was established in 1953 after the corrupt régime of King Farouk had been toppled by a military coup. Since 1958, the flag of Egypt has been a red, white and black tricolor, although the emblem in the centre has varied. The current design has a gold eagle emblem symbolizing Saladin, the hero who led the Arabs in the 12th century. The colours signify pan-African unity.

Population: 55,745,000	**Capital:** *Cairo*
Languages: *Arabic*	**Currency:** *Egyptian pound*

Equatorial Guinea

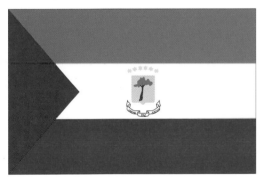

Equatorial Guinea is situated in West Africa and is comprised of a mainland area called Mbini and five mountainous and volcanic islands. The capital Malabo is on the largest of the islands, which is called Bioko. The country was one of the last African countries to achieve independence, which took place in 1968. The flag was altered during the dictatorship of Francisco Nguema (1972-1979) but has now been restored to its 1968 form. The emblem depicts a silk cotton tree and six stars representing the mainland and islands. Green represents the country's natural resources, blue the sea, red the struggle for freedom, and white for peace.

Population: 447,000	**Capital:** *Malabo*
Languages: *Spanish,*	**Currency:** *Franc C.F.A.*

Eritrea

Eritrea was a colony of Italy until 1941, then was administered by the British military until 1952 when it became an autonomous region within the Federation of Ethiopia and Eritrea. After a long struggle, on 24 May 1993, Eritrea declared independence and broke away from Ethiopia. The new flag was a variation on the flag of the Eritrean People's Liberation Front. The flag features an olive wreath which was taken from an older flag used between 1952 and 1959.

Population: 3,670,000	**Capital:** *Asmera*
Languages: *Tigrinya*	**Currency:** *Ethiopian birr in use*

Ethiopia

Ethiopia is a mountainous country and features part of the Great Rift Valley. The Blue Nile and its tributaries originate here. Ethiopia suffers from periods of severe drought. Until 1936 it was the only African country not conquered by the Europeans until Italy invaded and ruled until 1941. After British troops forced the Italians out, Emperor Haile Selassie ruled the country until 1974 when he was deposed by a military coup. Ethiopia was declared a socialist state and President Mengistu took control in 1977 with a period of 'Red Terror'. The military régime collapsed in 1991, and Ethiopia is now working towards a democratic federal system of government. The flag first appeared in 1897. The Ethiopian flag has become the basis for many other African flags signifying pan-Africanism.

Population: 51,831,000	**Capital:** *Addis Ababa*
Languages: *Amharic*	**Currency:** *Birr*

Gabon

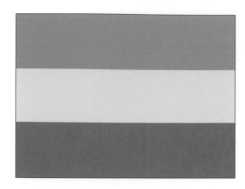

Gabon lies on the equator in West Africa and took its name from a 16th century Portuguese explorer called Gabāo. The climate is humid and hot with a high rainfall, and has rich forest and mineral resources. Gabon was a French colony from the 1880s until independence in 1960 when the flag was first adopted. The yellow stripe representing the sun perhaps also symbolizes the equator. The green stripe stands for the forest and the blue for the sea.

Population: 1,235,000	Capital: Libreville
Languages: French	Currency: Franc C.F.A.

The Gambia

The Gambia is a very small country and lies in the far west of Africa. It is a long, narrow, country which follows the course of the River Gambia. The country is almost completely surrounded by Senegal. Once part of the great Mali empire, it became involved in the slave trade after the arrival of the Portuguese in the 15th century. They were supplanted by the British who made this a colony in 1843. Independence came in 1965 and with it the flag, as we now see it, was adopted. The blue stripes symbolize the river Gambia, the red the sun overhead and green for the land.

Population: 1,019,000	Capital: Banjul
Languages: English,	Currency: Dalasi

Ghana

The west African country of Ghana faces the Gulf of Guinea with its southern coast on the Atlantic Ocean. In the 17th century the area became a centre of the slave trade which lasted until the 1860s. Formerly known as the Gold Coast, the country took the name Ghana in 1957 when the country became independent. The flag, adopted in 1957, is red, yellow and green. These are the pan-African colours which signify African unity. These colours were first used by Ethiopia, the oldest independent nation in Africa. The black star represents African freedom.

Population: 16,261,000	Capital: Accra
Languages: English	Currency: Cedi

Guinea

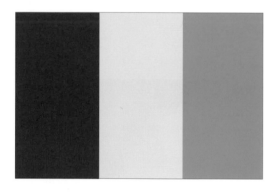

Guinea is a country of varied landscapes facing the Atlantic Ocean in West Africa. The flag was first introduced shortly after independence from France in 1958. Guinea's flag is based on the French tricolor, but uses the pan-African colours. The colours represent the three words of the national motto 'Travail, Justice, Solidarity': red for work, yellow for justice and green for solidarity.

Population: 6,269,000	Capital: Conakry
Languages: French	Currency: Guinea franc

Guinea-Bissau

Lying between Guinea and Senegal in West Africa, Guinea-Bissau is a small, low-lying, tropical country with a swampy coastal area. It has many offshore islands. Guinea-Bissau was once known as Portuguese Guinea and was ruled by the Portuguese for 500 years until independence in 1973. The flag has adopted the pan-African colours. The five-pointed star indicates African freedom. The flag is very similar to the flag adopted by Cape Verde, but now superseded. Both flags derived from that of the *Partido Africano da Independencia da Guine e Cabo Verde* (PAIGC; African Party for the Independence of Guinea and Cape Verde).

Population: 1,043,000	Capital: Bissau
Languages: Portuguese	Currency: Guinea-Bissau peso

Kenya

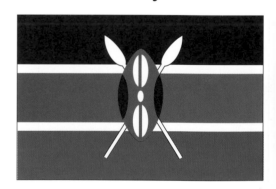

An equatorial country, Kenya lies in East Africa on the Indian Ocean. The climate is tropical. Kenya has been a centre for trading for thousands of years. The area has been influenced by Arabs, Portuguese and the British who took over in 1895. Kenya became independent in 1963 when the flag was adopted. It is based on the Kenya African National Union flag, which organization led the movement towards independence from the British. The central image is a Masai warrior's shield with crossed spears.

Population: 25,376,000	Capital: Nairobi
Languages: English, Swahili	Currency: Kenya shilling

Lesotho

The Kingdom of Lesotho is a small, mountainous country with the River Orange running through it. The climate makes agriculture difficult, although most of the population survives through subsistence farming. Many people try to find work in neighbouring South Africa. The country was a British protectorate from 1868, until 1966 when it became independent. In 1986 the leader of the Lesotho National Party was deposed and new military rulers took over the country. A year later, the new flag was adopted. Parliamentary elections were held in 1993. The white, blue and green signify the words of the national motto Khotso, Pula, Nala (Peace, Rain, Plenty). The emblem is composed of shield, knobkerrie, spear and ostrich feather sceptre.

Population: *1,899,000*	Capital: *Maseru*
Languages: *Sesotho, English*	Currency: *Loti*

Liberia

Liberia is situated in West Africa. The country is sparsely populated and mainly tropical rain forest. Liberia, as the name suggests, was founded as an American colony for freed black slaves in 1821-1822. This became the first new independent state of modern Africa, when independence was declared in 1847. The flag derives from the American Stars and Stripes. Its eleven red and white stripes represent the 11 men who signed the declaration of independence. The single white star symbolizes the 'shining light in the dark continent'. Since 1989, Liberia has been heavily involved in civil war.

Population: *2,373,000*	Capital: *Monrovia*
Languages: *English,*	Currency: *Liberian dollar*

Libya

Libya is a large country bordering the Mediterranean Sea. It has a harsh, arid climate and much of the country is desert, although the coastal area is more fertile. Libya was controlled by the Italians from 1912 until they were defeated in World War II. In 1969, the monarchy of Libya were overthrown by a coup led by Colonel Gaddafi. The plain green flag represents the country's commitment to the 'green revolution' in agriculture and to Islam. The uniform colour symbolizes the equality of all citizens.

Population: *5,039,000*	Capital: *Tripoli*
Languages: *Arabic*	Currency: *Libyan dinar*

Madagascar

Madagascar is a large island situated off the east coast of Africa. Because of its size, Madagascar has a varied climate ranging from arid to hot and wet. Once occupied by the French, the island still retains much of its French influence. Since gaining independence in 1958, the country continued its links with France until it became a socialist dictatorship in 1975. It was only in 1991 that this régime was defeated. Presidential elections took place in 1992/1993, but the country remains very poor. The white, red and green of Madagascar's flag originates from the colours of many south-east Asian countries. Despite its proximity to Africa, Madagascar is largely populated by Malayo-Polynesians. The flag was adopted in 1958 when the country first became independent.

Population: *12,728,000*	Capital: *Antananarivo*
Languages: *Malagasy,* *French*	Currency: *Malagasy franc*

Malawi

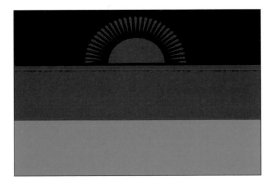

Malawi is a small country by African standards. A British protectorate under the name Nyasaland from 1891, the country gained independence from Britain in 1964 and the Malawi Congress Party, led by Dr. Hastings Kamuzu Banda, took over control. In 1971 Dr. Banda declared himself president for life. Under his control, Malawi saw brief periods of growth, but the country remains predominantly very poor. Banda was defeated in elections in 1994 and was replaced as President by Bakili Muluzi. The flag dates back to 1953 when the Malawi Congress Party was first established. The rising sun symbolizes the dawning of a new era and the colours are those of the Black Liberation Movement.

Population: *9,303,000*	Capital: *Lilongwe*
Languages: *English*	Currency: *Malawian kwacha*

Mali

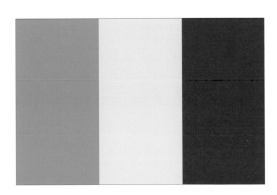

Mali is a poor, landlocked country in West Africa. Much of the country lies within the Sahara Desert, making the population extremely reliant upon the Senegal and Niger rivers for their survival. Mali became independent from France in 1960 but soon became dominated by the repressive rule of Moussa Traoré. Mali became free of this régime in 1991, after a revolution. The flag dates back to 1959 and is made up of the pan-African colours, symbolizing African unity. Originally, the centre of the flag featured a stylized figure. However, this was dropped in 1961.

Population: *9,234,000*	Capital: *Bamako*
Languages: *French*	Currency: *Franc C.F.A.*

Mauritania

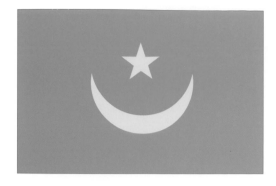

Much of Mauritania is covered by the Sahara Desert. Agriculture is based mainly along the Senegal River. In recent years, persistent drought was devastated the herds the of nomadic population. Originally part of French West Africa, Mauritania became fully independent in 1960. The flag was introduced in 1959, a year prior to independence. The green background to the flag with the yellow crescent and star are all traditional symbols of the Islamic religion.

Population: 2,137,000	Capital: *Nouakchott*
Languages: *Arabic*	Currency: *Ouguiya*

Mauritius

Mauritius lies off the east African coast and consists of the main island with many reefs and smaller islets in the vicinity. Mauritius was settled by the Dutch in 1639, followed by the French and then the British. It finally became independent in 1968 when the flag was first adopted. Its colours – red, blue, yellow and green – are those of the coat of arms dating back to 1906. Red stands for the struggle for independence, blue for the Indian Ocean, yellow for the bright future and sunlight, and green is for the vegetation and agriculture of the country.

Population: 1,111,000	Capital: *Port Louis*
Languages: *English*	Currency: *Mauritius rupee*

Morocco

Morocco occupies the north-western corner of Africa. Peasant agriculture and nomadic pastoralism make up much of the economy, although in recent years, tourism has become increasingly more important. Morocco has been ruled by the Sharifian dynasty since the 16th century, though Spain laid claim to coastal settlements which became enclaves in the 19th century. In 1912, it became a French protectorate with areas controlled by Spain until 1956 when it gained independence. Originally, Morocco's flag was plain red like many other Arab countries and dates back to the 16th century. The green star, 'Solomon's Seal' was added in 1915, and is a religious emblem.

Population: 26,721,000	Capital: *Rabat*
Languages: *Arabic*	Currency: Moroccan *dirham*

Mozambique

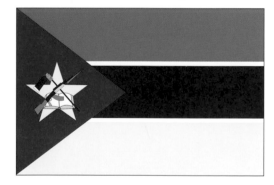

Mozambique lies in south-east Africa. The climate is tropical. After breaking ties with Portugal in 1975 the country was plunged into civil war accompanied by a series of droughts and floods. As a consequence the country remains poor. The colours of the flag derive from the colours used in the flag of the Frelimo party. This was the organization which led the struggle for independence from the Portuguese. Frelimo won a majority of seats in multiparty elections held in 1994. The former guerrilla group, Renamo, came second in the election. The current flag was adopted in 1983 and is more closely based on the original Frelimo flag. The green represents the land, the black stripe Africa and the yellow stripe mineral wealth. The red triangle has a badge featuring the rifle, hoe, cog-wheel and book. These are all Marxist symbols for the fight for independence against colonialism. Mozambique relinquished its Marxist policies in 1989.

Population: 16,916,000	Capital: *Maputo*
Languages: *Portuguese*	Currency: *Metical*

Namibia

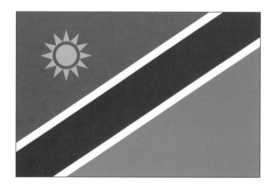

Namibia occupies a large area in the south-west corner of Africa. With rich natural resources, the country has a varied landscape ranging from desert coastline to mountain regions. Apart from a minor British influence, the majority of the country was under German control as a protectorate from 1884. During World War I, Namibia was taken out of German control and placed in the hands of the Union of South Africa at the request of the Allies. It was not until 1990 that the country achieved full independence. The flag is very new, dating only from 1990, and is derived from the flag of SWAPO (South-West Africa People's Organization), who led the struggle against the South African occupation of Namibia. The green, blue and gold sun represents the natural resources of the country, with the red and the white symbolizing the people.

Population: 1,565,000	Capital: *Windhoek*
Languages: *English*	Currency: *Namibian dollar*

Niger

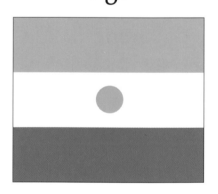

Niger is a large, landlocked African country. With desert to the north and a substantial mountainous area, only a small proportion of the area where the River Niger flows is cultivable. Like Nigeria, the country is named after the river through which it flows. Niger was formerly a French colony but achieved independence in 1960. The flag dates back to 1959. The orange stripe represents the desert, the white unity and the purity of the people. The orange disc represents the sun and the green stripe the Niger Valley.

Population: 8,440,000	Capital: *Niamey*
Languages: *French*	Currency: *Franc C.F.A.*

Nigeria

Situated on the West African coast, Nigeria is a large, highly populated country. With a terrain ranging from tropical rain forest, savanna and mountains to mangrove swamps and sandy beaches, Nigeria is extremely varied. It was a British colony between 1914 and 1960. From 1967 to 1970, Nigeria experienced a bitter civil war when the Ibo people of Biafra in Nigeria's eastern region declared independence, but were defeated. The flag was adopted in 1960 and was the result of a winning entry in a competition. The green represents the country's agriculture and forests and the white peace.

Population: 104,893,000	**Capital:** *Abuja Federal District*
Languages: *English,*	**Currency:** *Naira*

Rwanda

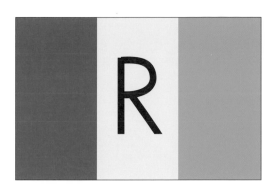

Rwanda is a small, landlocked country. The population is dense and very poor relying mainly on agriculture. Rwanda was part of German East Africa, but during World War I was occupied by Belgium and became the UN Trust Territory of Ruanda-Urundi. Rwanda finally achieved independence in 1962. The southern part of Ruanda-Urundi is now Burundi. Since independence, fierce conflict between the country's two main ethnic groups, the Hutu and the Tutsi, has seriously damaged the country's development. The flag was adopted in 1961 and features the pan-African colours signifying African unity. To avoid confusion with Guinea's flag the R was added, which stands for Rwanda, referendum and revolution.

Population: 7,490,000	**Capital:** *Kigali*
Languages: *French,*	**Currency:** *Rwanda franc*
Kinyarwanda	

São Tomé & Principe

The state consists of two small islands in the Gulf of Guinea. They are mountainous, volcanic and heavily forested. These islands became a Portuguese colony in 1522 and gained their independence in 1975. Dating from independence the flag has the traditional pan-African colours signifying African unity and is based on the flag used by the national liberation movement prior to independence. The two black stars represent the two islands.

Population: 125,000	**Capital:** *São Tomé*
Languages: *Portuguese*	**Currency:** *Dobra*

Senegal

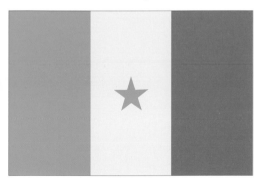

Senegal is situated in the far west of Africa. Dakar is by far the largest city and industrial centre. Senegal was France's oldest colony and became the administrative centre for French West Africa. A year prior to independence in 1960, Senegal joined the Federation of Mali and the two countries adopted a joint flag. However, after independence the two countries went their separate ways and an attempted federation with Gambia in 1981-1989 also failed. Mali kept the old flag, but that of Senegal is very similar, with a green five-pointed star symbolizing the Muslim faith. The colours of the flag were originally chosen to show solidarity with Ghana.

Population: 8,054,000	**Capital:** *Dakar*
Languages: *French*	**Currency:** *Franc C.F.A.*

Seychelles

The Seychelles consists of over 100 islands in the Indian Ocean, many of which are uninhabited. The country was a French colony from 1756 and British from 1814. On independence in 1976, the Seychelles adopted a flag that combined the colours of the two leading political parties, the Democrats and the Seychelles People's United Party. However, one year later, the Peoples' United Party seized power. The flag introduced at this time, symbolizes the Indian Ocean in its white wavy stripe, the green is for agriculture and the red for revolution and economic progress.

Population: 70,000	**Capital:** *Victoria*
Languages: *Creole, English*	**Currency:** *Seychelles rupee*
French	

Sierra Leone

Situated on the coast of West Africa, Sierra Leone has a hot, tropical, climate. It has swampy areas near the coast and high mountains and plateaus in the interior. Sierra Leone means 'The Lion Mountains' and like Liberia, was intended to be a home for freed slaves when it was founded by British philanthropists in 1787, the capital being named Freetown. A British colony from 1808, Sierra Leone became independent in 1961 when the new flag was introduced. The colours of the flag derive from the country's coat of arms. The green stands for agriculture, the white for unity and peace and the blue for the Atlantic Ocean.

Population: 4,468,000	**Capital:** *Freetown*
Languages: *English*	**Currency:** *Leone*

Somali Republic

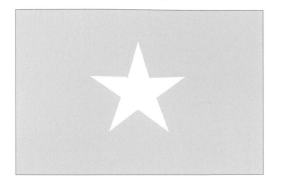

The Somali Republic, or Somalia as it is also known, is situated partly on the Gulf of Aden and also on the Indian Ocean. The country was ruled by both the British and Italians with independence arriving in 1960 when the two European colonies united. The flag takes its colours from that of the United Nations. The five-pointed star represents the five main regions where the Somalis live, those being northern Kenya, Ethiopia, French Somaliland (now Djibouti), British Somaliland and Italian Somaliland. The star itself represents African freedom.

Population: *8,543,000*	**Capital:** *Mogadishu*
Languages: *Somali, Arabic*	**Currency:** *Somali shilling*

South Africa

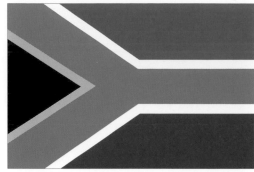

South Africa came into existence as a result of a union in 1910 between Boer (Afrikaner) and British territories following two and a half centuries of European settlement and conquest. Domination of the black population began early, resulting in the introduction of apartheid in 1948 when discrimination and racial segregation was stringently enforced. However, in 1989, reforms began with multiracial elections being held in 1994 and a new black president, Nelson Mandela, was elected. At this time, the new flag was introduced. The flag combines the colours of the European peoples (red, white and blue) with the colours of the African National Congress (black, yellow and green).

Population: *40,677,000*	**Capital:** *Pretoria,*
Languages: *Afrikaans,*	*Cape Town, Bloemfontein*
English, African languages	**Currency:** *Rand*

Sudan

Sudan is the largest country in Africa and consists mainly of great plains. It includes part of the Nile basin and Sahara Desert. Much of the country is uninhabited, with the majority of the population living by the waters of the White and the Blue Niles. In 1956, Sudan became independent from Britain and Egypt who had ruled since 1889. However, since independence ,the country has been plunged into civil wars between the Muslims in the north and the non-Muslim population in the south. The flag was adopted in 1969, the main feature being the pan-Arab colours, with an Islamic green triangle. The flag was a winning entry in a competition.

Population *27,255,000*	**Capital:** *Khartoum*
Languages: *Arabic*	**Currency:** *Sudanese dinar*

Swaziland

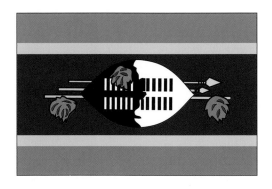

Swaziland is a small, landlocked country in southern Africa with a varied landscape. In 1902, Britain took control of the country, which remained British until 1968 when the country achieved independence. Swaziland has a very distinctive flag which was adopted on independence. The design is based on one designed for the Swazi Pioneer Corps in 1941 and is therefore related to flags used in the British Army. The emblems are pure Swazi and show the weapons of a warrior – ox-hide shield, two assegai (spears) and a fighting stick.

Population: *888,000*	**Capital:** *Mbabane*
Languages: *English, Swazi*	**Currency:** *Lilangeni*

Tanzania

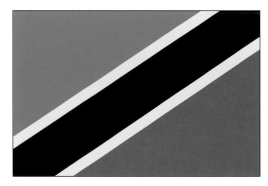

Tanzania is situated across the high plateau of eastern Africa where the extinct volcano of Kilimanjaro, the highest mountain in Africa, is to be found. The country of Tanzania dates from 1964 when the two countries of Tanganyika and Zanzibar united. The flag of Tanzania has adopted the colours of these former countries. Green is representative of agricultural resources, green for mineral wealth, while black is for the people with blue representing water and Zanzibar.

Population: *26,743,000*	**Capital:** *Dodoma*
Languages: *English, Swahili*	**Currency:** *Tanzanian shilling*

Togo

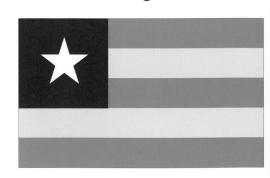

Togo is situated in West Africa and stretches north from the Gulf of Guinea. The first Europeans to reach Togo were the Portuguese in the late 15th century and it later became important in the slave trade. In 1884, the country was colonized by Germany, although after World War I, the territory was occupied by the French and the British. Later, the British sector became part of Ghana and the French became independent in 1960 as Togo. Based on the stars and stripes, Togo's flag has the pan-African colours representing African unity. Green represents agriculture, red, bloodshed, yellow, the mineral resources, while white is for purity. The five stripes symbolize the five administrative areas of Togo.

Population: *4,026,000*	**Capital:** *Lomé*
Languages: *French*	**Currency:** *C.F.A.*

Tunisia

Tunisia is the smallest country in North Africa and on the Mediterranean Coast. It has a long and varied history with strong influences from the Arabs, Turks, Romans, and later from the French who ruled Tunisia from 1881 to 1956. The flag features the five-pointed star and the crescent moon, both of which symbolize Islam. Dating from 1835, the flag is based on the Turkish flag, but was not officially adopted until 1923.

Population: 8,609,000		**Capital:** *Tunis*	
Languages: *Arabic*		**Currency:** *Tunisian dinar*	

Uganda

The Republic of Uganda is a landlocked country in East Africa and contains part of Lake Victoria. In the south, Uganda has rain forests, while the north is less wet with savanna and grassland. The British took over the country in 1894 and ruled it until independence in 1962. The years following independence saw a succession of civil wars, violence and massacres. The flag was adopted in 1962 and is based on the colours of the Uganda People's Congress which was in power at the time of independence. Black represents the people, yellow, the sun and red is for brotherhood. In the centre of the flag is the country's emblem: the red crested crane.

Population 18,026,000	**Capital:** *Kampala*
Languages: *Swahili, English*	**Currency:** *Shilling*

Zäire

Zäire extends over a large area, much of which lies in the drainage basin on the River Zäire, formerly the River Congo. Dense rainforests grow in the north with savanna to the south. Zäire, a possession of the Belgian crown in 1885 was a colony from 1908 until it gained independence in 1960. The pan-African colours, signifying African unity, were adopted for the flag in 1971. The emblem in the centre of the flag was used by the Movement of the Revolution, formed in 1967. The green field represents hope for the future. This is the third flag since independence.

Population: 40,997,000	**Capital:** *Kinshasa*
Languages: *French*	**Currency:** *Zaire*

Zambia

For the first half of the 20th century, when it was controlled first by the British South Africa Company and then became a colony, Zambia was known as Northern Rhodesia. It contains a large area of high plateaus and is situated in south-central Africa. The Victoria Falls lie on its border with Zimbabwe. The flag dates from independence from Britain in 1964 when the name Zambia was adopted. The orange stands for the mineral resources of the country, the black for the people and the red for the struggles of the country. The soaring eagle represents freedom and independence and the green background is for agriculture and forestry.

Population: 8,527,000	**Capital:** *Lusaka*
Languages: *English*	**Currency:** Zambian *kwacha*

Zimbabwe

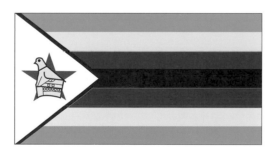

Zimbabwe is situated in south-central Africa and is covered with vast areas of grassland. Britain colonized Zimbabwe in 1894, naming it Southern Rhodesia. Independence would have come in 1963 if the white settlers had attempted majority rule. When refused they declared independence unilaterally. International sanctions had less effect on the white administration than escalating guerrilla action, until eventually, black majority rule was accepted and an independent Zimbabwe was created in 1980. The flag was adopted on legal independence in 1980, the colours of the flag being taken from the ruling Patriotic Front.

Population: 10,638,000	**Capital:** *Harare*
Languages: *English*	**Currency:** Zimbabwe dollar

The Victoria Falls - Zimbabwe

Australasia
& the
Pacific

1. Australia
2. Fiji
3. Kiribati
4. Marshall Islands
5. Micronesia
6. Nauru
7. New Zealand
8. Palau (Belau)
9. Papua and New Guinea
10. Solomon Islands
11. Tonga
12. Tuvalu
13. Vanuatu
14. Western Samoa

Dependency
15. American Samoa
16. Cook Islands
17. French Polynesia
18. New Caledonia
19. Nuie
20. Northern Mariana Islands
21. Tokelau
22. Wallis and Futuna Islands

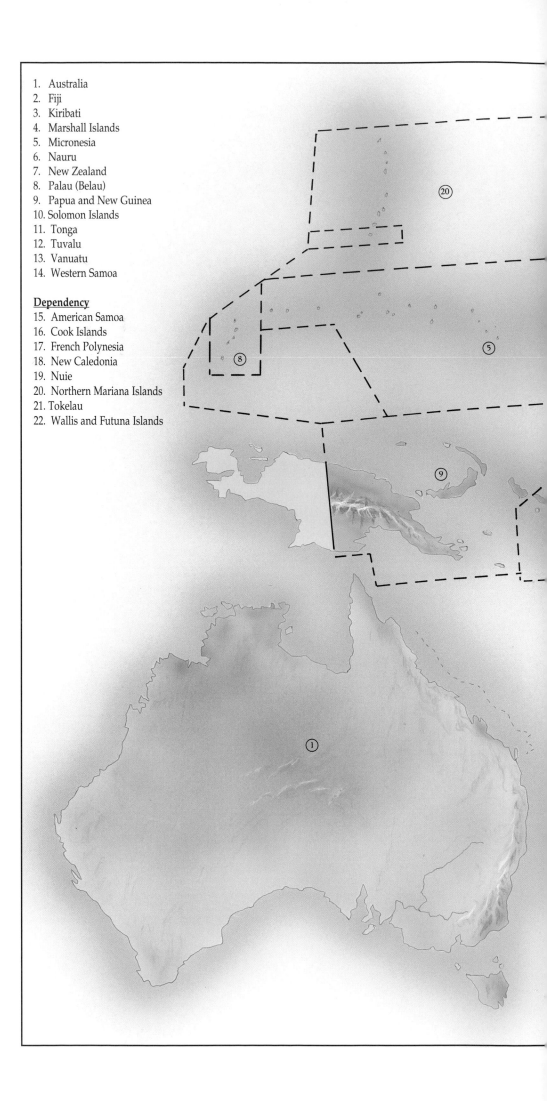

Pilbara Outback station – Western Australia

Australia

A vast country largely made up of desert and semi-desert, with the majority of the population living in coastal areas, Australia has a fascinating geography. Australia's flag was adopted in 1901, the result of a winning entry in a competition. Clearly showing Australia's links with Britain, the flag features the blue ensign. The star formation represents the constellation of the Southern Cross; this emblem has been used to symbolize the continent since its very early days. The larger seven point star known as the Commonwealth Star, symbolizes the six states and the territories. A separate flag for Australia's Aboriginal people was introduced in 1972.

Fiji

Fiji consists of more than 300 Melanesian islands which were discovered in 1643 by the Dutch explorer Abel Tasman. Fiji became a British Crown Colony in 1874 and it took nearly 100 years for Fiji to gain its independence in 1970. The flag is clearly based on the blue ensign, but has a paler background than the traditional flag. The coat of arms shows a British lion, sugar cane, a coconut palm, bananas and a dove of peace.

Kiribati

Situated in the Pacific Ocean, Kiribati is made up of groups of coral atolls. The islands are very poor and over-crowded and thus dependent on foreign aid. Previously known as the Gilbert Islands, the name was changed to Kiribati on independence from Britain in 1979. The flag shows the arms granted to the Gilbert and Ellice Islands in 1937. They consists of a yellow frigate bird above a sun rising over the Pacific Ocean.

Population: 17,707,000	Capital: *Canberra*
Languages: *English*	Currency: *Australian dollar*

Population: 759,000	Capital: *Suva*
Languages: *English*	Currency: *Fiji dollar*

Population: 76,000	Capital: *Tarawa*
Languages: *English*	Currency: *Australian dollar*

The koala bear is one of Australia's most famous animals

Marshall Islands

The Marshall Islands comprise an archipelago of over 1,000 islands and atolls. Between 1946 and 1958, the U.S.A. tested 64 nuclear weapons on the islands of Bikini and Enewetak, and it is thought that the local population is still suffering from the effects. Once a German protectorate, the Marshall Islands were occupied by the Japanese during World War II but became administered by the U.S.A. as part of the UN Trust Territory of the Pacific from 1947. The islands became a republic 'in free association with the U.S.A.' in 1986. The country is still heavily dependent upon U.S. aid.

Population: *53,000*	**Capital:** *Majuro*
Languages: *English*	**Currency:** *U.S. dollar*

Micronesia

The Federated States of Micronesia is an archipelago of islands comprising most of the Caroline Islands in the Pacific Ocean. It is a federated state in free association with the U.S.A. and gained its present status in 1985. The flag dates from to 1962. The two colours – white and light blue – are the colours of the UN. The four stars stand for the four states (Kosrai, Pohnpei, Truk and Yap).

Population: *110,000*	**Capital:** *Palikir*
Languages: *English*	**Currency:** *U.S. dollar*

Nauru

Situated in the middle of the Pacific Ocean, Nauru is a coral atoll lying just south of the equator. It achieved independence in 1968 after being under a UN trusteeship since 1946. The country is dependent upon the export of phosphate rock which will be eventually depleted. The flag was the winner in a design competition. The 12-pointed star represents the aboriginal people of the island. The star is situated under the yellow line (the equator) representing the location of the country in the Pacific Ocean.

Population: *10,000*	**Capital:** *none*
Languages: *English*	**Currency:** *Australian dollar*

New Zealand

Situated in the Pacific Ocean, New Zealand is a mountainous country lying on a belt of tectonic activity. It was settled by Maoris in the 8th century, though they may not have been the first inhabitants. The first European to discover it was Abel Tasman in 1642. Its coasts were charted by James Cook in 1769-1770. Britain aimed to take control of the country claiming the South Island by right of discovery and the North Island by the Treaty of Weitangi with Maori chiefs in 1840. New Zealand took Dominion status in 1907 with full independence in 1931. The flag dates from 1869. It features the British blue ensign and has a stylized version of the Southern Cross constellation displaying four of the five stars.

Population: *3,462,000*	**Capital:** *Wellington*
Languages: *English, Maori*	**Currency:** *New Zealand dollar*

Palau (Belau)

Palau (Belau) comprises 26 islands and 300 islets. The islands are mainly mountainous reefs. The islands became independent in 1994. They were formerly part of the UN Trust Territory of the Pacific Islands and were under U.S. administration. The flag has an off-centre yellow disc depicting the moon. This represents national unity and destiny. The blue background stands for the achievement of independence.

Population: *15,000*	**Capital:** *Koror*
Languages: *English, Palauan*	**Currency:** *U.S. dollar*

Papua New Guinea

Papua New Guinea forms part of Melanesia and takes up the eastern part of the island of New Guinea and a large number of adjacent islands. European contact dates back to the 16th century. However, it was not until the 19th century that British and German settlers arrived. Papua New Guinea is in the Commonwealth having been ruled from after World War II until 1975 by Australia. It became fully independent in 1975, though the flag dates from 1971. The use of the five stars of the Southern Cross constellation is due to Australian influence. The bird of paradise is an emblem which goes back to the days of German rule and appeared on two previous flags.

Population: *4,148,000*	**Capital:** *Port Moresby*
Languages: *English*	**Currency:** *Kina*

Solomon Islands

Tonga

Tuvalu

The Solomon Islands lie in the Pacific Ocean, south-east of Papua New Guinea, and were British from 1893 until 1978 when they gained independence and the new flag was adopted. The five five-pointed stars on a background of blue represents the country's five main islands, surrounded by the Pacific Ocean. Green is for the forests and yellow for the sun. The flag was the winning entry in a design competition.

Situated in the southern Pacific Ocean, Tonga is an archipelago of at least 170 islands. Once a British protectorate, the islands became fully independent in 1970. The flag, dating back to 1875 and still in force, is based on the British red ensign. It is intended to represent the Christian faith of the nation. The red cross has now become Tonga's national emblem.

Tuvalu means 'The Eight Islands', although there are in fact nine main islands making up the country. Lying in the southern Pacific Ocean and settled by Polynesians since the 14th century, it was claimed by Britain in 1892. The islands became independent in 1978 when the flag was adopted. It is based on the blue ensign, but the background is a much paler blue. The nine golden stars represent the state's main islands.

Population: 346,000	Capital: *Honiara*
Languages: *English,*	Currency: *Solomon Islands dollar*

Population: 93,000	Capital: *Nuku'alofa*
Languages: *Tongan, English*	Currency: *Pa'anga*

Population: 9,500	Capital: *Fongafale*
Languages: *English, Tuvaluan*	Currency: *Australian dollar*

Vanuatu

Western Samoa

Vanuatu is a group of over 80 islands and islets in the Pacific Ocean. The islands were discovered by Europeans in 1606 by Captain Cook who named them the New Hebrides. From 1906, these islands were jointly administered by Britain and France but gained independence in 1980. On the flag, the Y represents the position of the islands within the sea. Within the angle of the Y is a boar's tusk and fern leaves representing war and peace. The colours of the flag are those of the political party who dominated events at the time of independence.

Western Samoa is made up of two large islands, with a number of other islands and islets situated in the Pacific Ocean. The islands were passed to Germany in 1899, although in 1920, they were taken over by New Zealand and finally achieved independence in 1962. The flag shows the Southern Cross constellation, a symbol linking Western Samoa to other countries in the southern hemisphere. The flag dates from 1948, prior to independence.

Population: 161,000	Capital: *Port-Vila*
Languages: *Bislama, English, French*	Currency: *Vatu*

Population: 163,000	Capital: *Apia*
Languages: *Samoan, English*	Currency: *Tala*

Sydney Opera House, Sydney, New South Wales, Australia

Populated Dependencies & Territories

Drangestad, Aruba

Abu Dhabi

Abu Dhabi is one of the seven sheikhdoms belonging to the United Arab Emirates. Abu Dhabi is an oil-rich country earning great wealth for its population. In 1952, these sheikhdoms came together as the Trucial States which was a British protectorate until 1971. There is one flag for the U.A.E., however, each emirate having its own flag except Sharjah. All the U.A.E. flags are in red and white.

Ajman

Ajman is a member of the United Arab Emirates and is the smallest, poorest member. Ajman has no oil and little industry and is largely supported by the other member states. The red and white flag is common to all of the U.A.E. states.

American Samoa

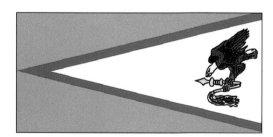

Placed in the South Pacific Ocean, American Samoa is a group of volcanic islands and atolls. Tutuila is the largest island in the group. Once divided between Germany and Britain, the islands were acquired by the United States in 1899, but the flag was not adopted until 1960. The flag shows the American eagle holding a Samoan war club and a tribal chief's staff, both symbols of the chief's authority.

Population: *798,000*   Capital: *Abu Dhabi*
Languages: *Arabic*   Currency: *U.A.E. dirham*

Population: *76,000*   Capital: *Ajman*
Languages: *Arabic*   Currency: *U.A.E. dirham*

Population: *53,000*   Capital: *Pago Pago*
Languages: *English, Samoan*   Currency: *U.S. dollar*

Anguilla

Anguilla is a long, thin, atoll and is part of the Lesser Antilles, or Leeward Islands. Together with the Virgin Islands, it is governed under one colonial administration by a British appointed Governor. The flag is the British blue ensign. In the shield are three dolphins which stand for strength, unity and endurance. White is for peace and blue for the sea.

Population: *9,000*	**Capital:** *The Valley*
Languages: *English*	**Currency:** *East Caribbean dollar*

Aruba

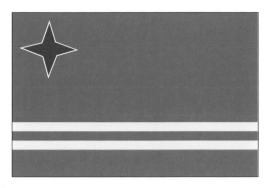

Aruba is a dry limestone island in the Lesser Antilles. It is a Dutch overseas territory, although, in 1986, it achieved separate status from the other Dutch islands in the area and now has complete internal control. The flag dates from 1976 and shows a four-pointed star representing the island's four main languages.

Population: *67,000*	**Capital:** *Oranjestad*
Languages: *Dutch,*	**Currency:** *Aruba Florin*
Papamiento	*(=Netherlands Antilles guilder)*

Azores

Situated in the North Atlantic Ocean, the Azores are made up of nine islands and are part of the mid-Atlantic ridge and volcanic in origin. The Azores have been a dependency of Portugal since 1430, although, in 1976, they were granted a greater degree of autonomy. The flag dates from 1979 and shows a hawk (or acor) after which the islands were named. The nine stars above the hawk represent the nine islands.

Population: *238,000*	**Capital:** *Ponta Delgada*
Languages: *Portuguese*	**Currency:** *Portuguese escudo*

Bermuda

First discovered by the the Spanish explorer Juan Bermudez, after whom the islands were named, Bermuda is Britain's oldest dependency and has been since 1609. Although the blue ensign is the typical flag of the British colonies, Bermuda flies the red ensign, with the shield of its coat of arms on the fly. The coat of arms shows a red lion holding another shield in which the shipwreck of the *Sea Venture* in 1609 is shown.

Population: *62,000*	**Capital:** *Hamilton*
Languages: *English*	**Currency:** *Bermuda dollar*
	(=U.S. dollar)

Cayman Islands

Situated north-west of Jamaica, the Cayman Islands is made up of three low-lying islands. The Caymans are a dependent territory of Britain and famous for offshore financial facilities. Tourism also plays an important part in the economy. The Cayman Islands fly the blue ensign, the coat of arms showing an English heraldic lion. The blue wavy lines symbolize the sea.

Population: *30,000*	**Capital:** *Georgetown*
Languages: *English*	**Currency:** *Cayman Island dollar*

Cook Islands

Named after Captain James Cook, these islands were a British protectorate from 1888 until 1901 when they became a dependency of New Zealand. The flag was adopted in 1979 and is a blue ensign. The fifteen stars represent the fifteen islands which make up the group.

Population: *18,600*	**Capital:** *Avarua*
Languages: *English*	**Currency:** *Cook Islands dollar*
	(=New Zealand dollar)

Dubai

Dubai is the second largest of the United Arab Emirates. The country was formerly one of the Trucial States before becoming part of the U.A.E. in 1971. The country is highly developed and modernized due to the country's oil wealth. The red and white flag is typical to the U.A.E. countries.

Population: *501,000*	**Capital:** *Dubai*	
Languages: *Arabic*	**Currency:** *U.A.E. dirham*	

Faeroe Islands

The Faeroe islands are situated in the North Atlantic, south-east of Iceland. The main industries are sheep farming and fishing. The islands are a dependency of Denmark and have been Danish since 1386 although in 1948 they became self-governing. The flag featuring the off-centre cross, is taken from the Danish flag. Red and blue are both traditional colours of the islands and white represents the foam of the sea.

Population: *48,000*	**Capital:** *Tórshavn*
Languages: *Danish*	**Currency:** *Danish Krone*

Falkland Islands

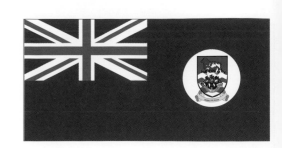

The Falkland Islands consist of two main islands lying off the coast of South America. The country was discovered in 1592 by John Davis. First populated by the French, then by the British, the islands were taken over by Argentina, but have been British since 1833. The Argentinians (who claim the islands and call them Las Malvinas) invaded the Falklands in 1982, but were defeated by the British. The flag is the blue ensign. The coat of arms within the disc shows John Davis' ship *Desire,* which discovered the islands. The sheep represent the main farming activity.

Population: *2,100*	**Capital:** Stanley
Languages: *English*	**Currency:** Falkland Pound (=Pound sterling)

French Guiana

French Guiana is the smallest country on the mainland of South America. The country has been a French dependency since 1676 and is treated as part of mainland France, being officially an Overseas Department and administrative region. The flag is the French tricolor.

Population: *133,000*	**Capital:** *Cayenne*
Languages: *French*	**Currency:** *French franc*

French Polynesia

French Polynesia is a group of 130 islands scattered halfway between Australia and South America. Tahiti is the largest island in the group. The islands became a French protectorate in 1843, but, in 1984, the islands gained increased internal control, though remaining an overseas territory.

Population: *213,000*	**Capital:** *Papeete*
Languages: *Papeete*	**Currency:** *French C.F.P* (*Communauté financiere pacifique*)

Fujairah

Fujairah is one of the smaller of the seven emirates that make up the United Arab Emirates. It is one of the poorer regions and it is the only emirate without a coastline on the Persian Gulf.

Population: *63,000*	**Capital:** *Fujairah*
Languages: *Arabic*	**Currency:** *U.A.E. dirham*

Gibraltar

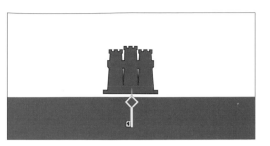

The Rock of Gibraltar lies at the north-eastern end of the Strait of Gibraltar. Gibraltar was first recognized as a British territory in 1713 and officially, its flag is the Union Jack. However since 1966 the flag showing the castle and key has been used internally. The castle represents Gibraltar's important strategic position on the Mediterranean, as does the key.

Population:	32,000	Capital:	Gibraltar
Languages:	English, Spanish	Currency:	Pound sterling

Greenland

Greenland is a large island in the Arctic with much of the land covered by a huge ice sheet (the world's second largest after Antarctica). The island has been a Danish possession since 1380 although full internal self-government was granted in 1981. The flag was introduced in 1985 as the result of a competition and reflects the colours of Denmark. The flag symbolizes the mid-summer sun rising over the polar ice.

Population:	57,000	Capital:	Nuuk (Godthab)
Languages:	Danish, Greenlandic	Currency:	Danish krone

Guadeloupe

Guadeloupe consists of seven islands in the Caribbean, the main islands being Basse-Terre, Grande-Terre, Saint-Martin and Saint-Barthélémy. Guadeloupe is a French Overseas Department and administrative region and therefore has the French tricolor as its flag.

Population:	405,000	Capital:	Basse-Terre
Languages:	French	Currency:	French franc

Guam

Guam is the largest of the Mariana group of islands lying in the western Pacific Ocean. The island was colonized by Spain in 1668 but became a dependency of the United States in 1898. The flag dates from 1917 and is flown alongside the 'Stars and Stripes'.

Population:	142,000	Capital:	Agana
Languages:	English, Chamorro	Currency:	U.S. dollar

Hong Kong

Hong Kong comprises Hong Kong Island and the surrounding smaller islands, the Kowloon peninsula and the 'New Territories'. Hong Kong is a British dependency and was acquired in stages. In 1898, Britain acquired a 99 year lease from the Chinese. This lease is due to expire in 1997 when Hong Kong will again become Chinese. The British blue ensign has been flying since 1841 when Hong Kong first became a British dependent territory. The flag shows the colony's coat of arms. The Chinese connection is represented by the dragon.

Population:	5,865,000	Capital:	Victoria
Languages:	Chinese, English	Currency:	Hong Kong dollar

Macao

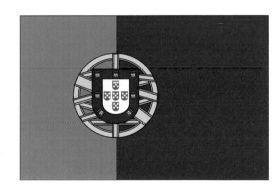

Macao is a Portuguese colony lying to the west of Hong Kong. In 1979, Macao was redefined as a Chinese territory under Portuguese Administration. It has also been agreed that the territory will be returned to China in 1999. Macao has been Portuguese since 1849.

Population:	391,000	Capital:	Macao
Languages:	Chinese, Portuguese	Currency:	Pataca

Madeira Islands

The Madeira Islands lie off the Moroccan coast in the Atlantic Ocean. The islands are a dependency of Portugal and were first discovered by João Goncalves Zarco in 1419. In 1980 the islands gained partial autonomy. The emblem on the flag dates back to the 15th century when the islands were first colonized. The cross represents the Order of Christ.

Population:	235,000	Capital:	Funchal
Languages:	Portuguese,	Currency:	Portuguese escudo

Martinique

Martinique forms a part of a group of volcanic islands lying in the Caribbean. Discovered by Columbus, the islands were colonized by the French from 1635. Martinique takes the French tricolor flag as it is an Overseas Department of France and also an administrative region.

Population:	369,000	Capital:	Fort-de-France
Languages:	French	Currency:	French franc

Montserrat

Montserrat is a volcanic island situated in the Carribean and was discovered by Columbus and then colonized by the Irish from 1632. Although it is a British Crown Colony, it became self-governing in 1960. The flag is the British blue ensign. The Irish influence is represented by the woman holding a harp. The woman also clasps a cross indicating Christianity.

Population:	12,000	Capital:	Plymouth
Languages:	English,	Currency:	East Caribbean dollar

Netherlands Antilles

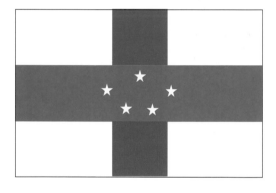

Lying in the Atlantic Ocean, the Netherlands Antilles are composed of five islands. In 1954, the dependency gained full self-government. Until 1986, Aruba was the sixth member of the island group when it broke away from Netherlands Antilles and gained complete internal autonomy.

Population:	196,000	Capital:	Willemstad
Languages:	Dutch,	Currency:	Netherlands Antilles
Papamiento, English			guilder

New Caledonia

New Caledonia is comprised of a series of islands in the Pacific Ocean. The islands have been a French possession since 1853 and an Overseas Territory since 1958. The flag is the French tricolor.

Population:	177,000	Capital:	Nouméa
Languages:	French	Currency:	French Franc

Niue Island

Niue Island is one of the Polynesian Islands which were annexed by New Zealand in 1901. It is a self-governing dependency of New Zealand. The flag shows the Union Jack with the addition of five stars. The yellow background symbolizes the warm relationship between Niue Island and New Zealand.

Population:	2,200	Capital:	Alofi
Languages:	English,	Currency:	New Zealand dollar
	Polynesian		

Norfolk Island

Halfway between New Caledonia and New Zealand, Norfolk Island was first discovered by Captain Cook in 1774. In 1914, it became a territory of the Australian Commonwealth. The island is known for its pine trees one of which is represented on its flag. The island is now a Territory of Australia.

Population:	2,000	Capital:	Kingston
Languages:	English	Currency:	Australian dollar

Northern Mariana Islands

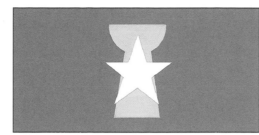

The Northern Mariana Islands lie in the Pacific Ocean and are a Commonwealth Territory of the U.S. From 1976, the Northern Marianas have had internal self-government. The flag dates from 1972. The grey shape in the centre of the flag is a latte stone, common to the islands. There is also a Polynesian Taga surrounded by a wreath of flowers and shells.

Population:	43,000	Capital:	Saipan
Languages:	English, Chamorro	Currency:	U.S. dollar

Pitcairn Islands

The Pitcairn Islands in the Pacific Ocean were first annexed by Britain in 1902 and are now a British Dependent Territory. The flag is the British blue ensign typical of most British overseas territories. The flag also displays the arms of the Islands.

Population:	65	Capital:	Kingstown
Languages:	English	Currency:	New Zealand dollar

Puerto Rico

First discovered by Columbus in 1493, Puerto Rico became Spanish in 1503 and it was then ceded to the U.S. in 1898. The island became self-governing in 1952. The flag derives from the U.S. 'Stars and Stripes' and is flown alongside the U.S. flag.

Population:	3,608,000	Capital:	San Juan
Languages:	English, Spanish	Currency:	U.S. dollar

Ras al-Khaimah

Ras Al-Khaimah is one of the sheikhdoms making up the United Arab Emirates. From 1952 to 1971, the sheikhdom was one of the Trucial States. The red and white colours of the flag are traditional to all the U.A.E. members.

Population:	130,000	Capital:	Ras al-Khaimah
Languages:	Arabic	Currency:	U.A.E. dirham

Réunion

Réunion is situated in the Indian Ocean and is the largest of the Mascarene Islands. The island is a French Overseas Department and administrative region and therefore flies the French tricolor.

Population:	620,000	Capital:	Saint-Denis
Languages:	French	Currency:	French franc

St. Helena Group

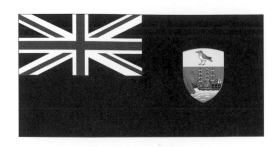

The St. Helena group of islands are situated in the southern Atlantic Ocean. British since 1834, the flag is the British blue ensign. The coat of arms in the fly shows a ship sailing towards the islands.

Population: 7,000	Capital: Jamestown
Languages: English,	Currency: Pound sterling

Turks & Caicos Islands

The Turks & Caicos Islands are situated in the Caribbean and have been British since 1766. The flag is the British blue ensign with the island's badge on the fly. It features a lobster, a shell and a Turk's head cactus.

Population: 12,000	Capital: Grand Turk
Languages: English	Currency: U.S. dollar

Umm al-Qaiwain

Situated on the Persian Gulf, Umm al-Qaiwain is one of the emirates making up the United Arab Emirates. The red and white flag is common to all U.A.E. members.

Population: 27,000	Capital: Umm al-Qaiwain
Languages: Arabic	Currency: U.A.E. dirham

Virgin Islands

The British Virgin Islands are part of the Lesser Antilles group and comprise four main islands. The islands have the British blue ensign, the badge showing a vestal virgin carrying a lamp. Beneath the shield is a gold scroll with the motto *Vigilate* 'Be Alert'.

The U.S. Virgin islands were first claimed as colonies by Spain, then became Danish and were finally sold to the U.S. in 1917. Dating from 1921, the flag derives from the seal of the U.S.A. The three arrows clutched by the eagle represent the three main islands. The letters 'V' and 'I' stand for Virgin Islands.

U.K. Virgin Islands
Population: 17,000	Capital: Road Town
Languages: English	Currency: U.S. dollar

U.S.A. Virgin Islands
Population: 99,000	Capital: Charlotte Amalie
Languages: English	Currency: U.S. dollar

National Museum, Georgetown, Cayman Islands.

St. John, Virgin Islands of the U.S.

States and Territories of Australia

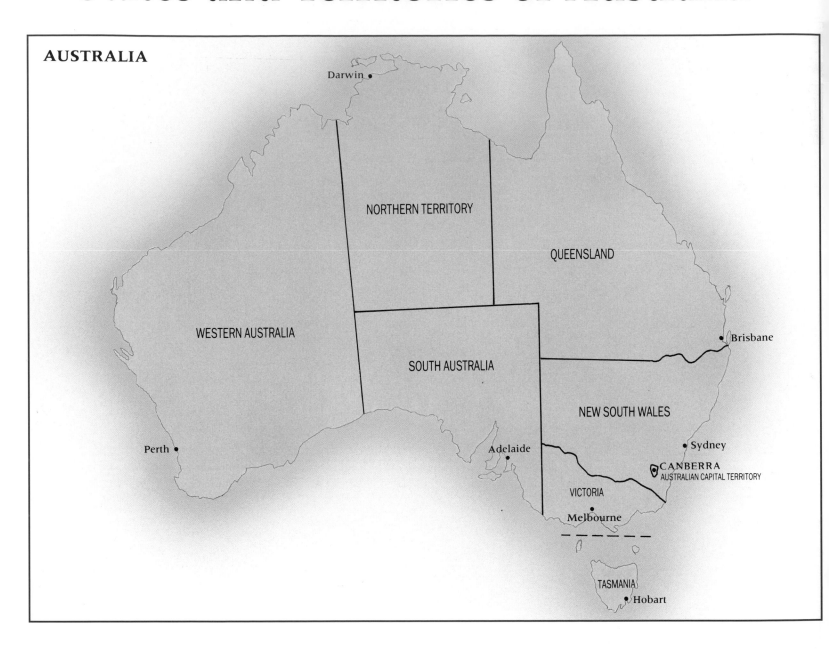

AUSTRALIA

Darwin

NORTHERN TERRITORY

QUEENSLAND

WESTERN AUSTRALIA

Brisbane

SOUTH AUSTRALIA

NEW SOUTH WALES

Perth

Adelaide

Sydney

CANBERRA
AUSTRALIAN CAPITAL TERRITORY

VICTORIA

Melbourne

TASMANIA

Hobart

New South Wales

Population: 6,000,000	Capital: Sydney

Northern Territory

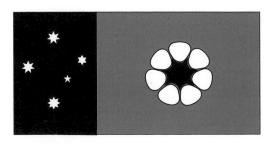

Population: 168,000	Capital: Darwin

Queensland

| Population: 3,095,000 | Capital: *Brisbane* |

South Australia

| Population: 1,460,000 | Capital: *Adelaide* |

Tasmania

| Population: 472,000 | Capital: *Hobart* |

Victoria

| Population: 4,461,000 | Capital: *Melbourne* |

Western Australia

| Population: 1,672,000 | Capital: *Perth* |

Ayers Rock, Australia

Provinces and Territories of Canada

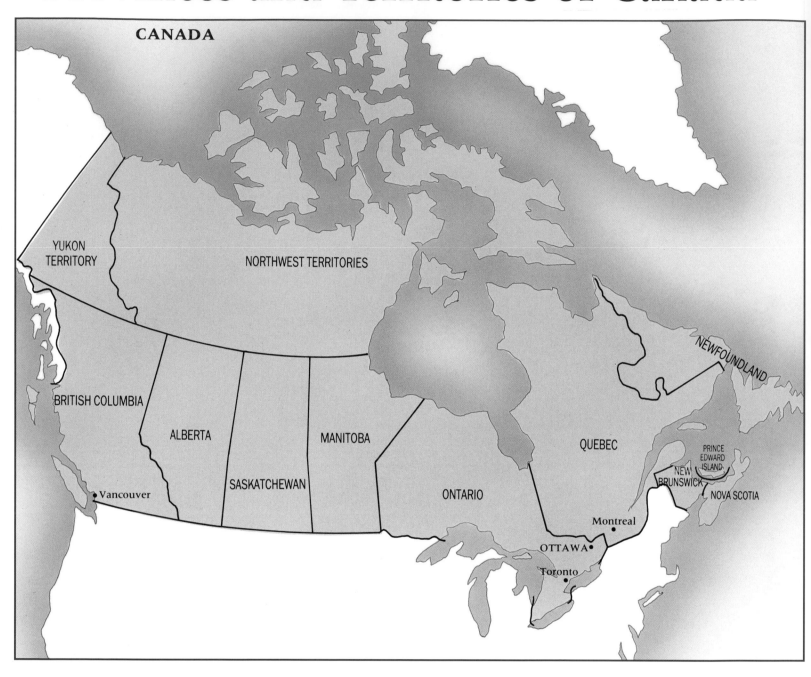

CANADA

YUKON TERRITORY

NORTHWEST TERRITORIES

NEWFOUNDLAND

BRITISH COLUMBIA

ALBERTA

SASKATCHEWAN

MANITOBA

ONTARIO

QUEBEC

NEW BRUNSWICK

PRINCE EDWARD ISLAND

NOVA SCOTIA

Vancouver

Montreal

OTTAWA

Toronto

Alberta

Population: *2,628,000*   Capital: *Edmonton*

British Columbia

Population: *3,446,000*   Capital: *Victoria*

Manitoba

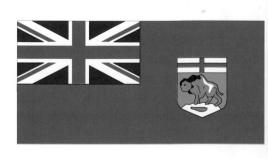

Population: *1,112,000*   Capital: *Winnipeg*

New Brunswick

Population: 749,000   Capital: *Fredericton*

Newfoundland

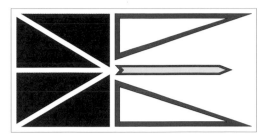

Population: 581,000   Capital: *St. John's*

Northwest Territories

Population: 62,000   Capital: *Yellowknife*

Nova Scotia

Population: 921,000   Capital: *Halifax*

Ontario

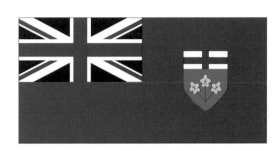

Population: 10,593,000   Capital: *Toronto*

Prince Edward Island

Population: 130,000   Capital: *Charlottestown*

Toronto skyline, as seen from Toronto Island, Canada

Quebec

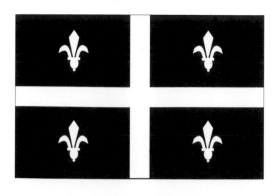

Population: 7,143,000   Capital: *Quebec*

Saskatchewan

Population: 1,004,000   Capital: *Regina*

Yukon Territory

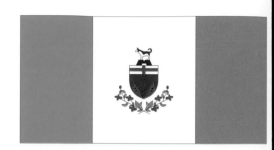

Population: 30,000   Capital: *Whitehorse*

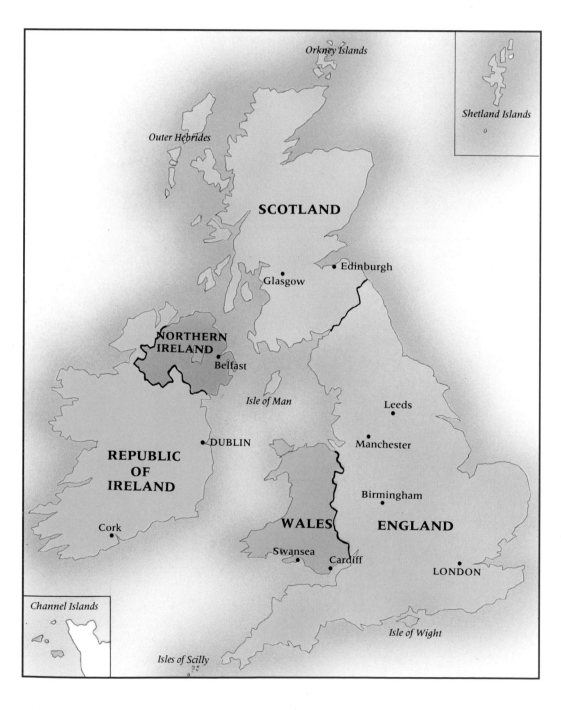

Divisions of the United Kingdom

England

Population: 48,373,000   Capital: *London*

Pulteney Bridge, Bath, Avon, England

Scotland

Population: 5,111,000   Capital: *Edinburgh*

Wales

Population: 2,899,000   Capital: *Cardiff*

Northern Ireland

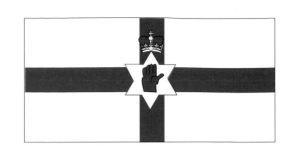

Population: 1,610,000   Capital: *Belfast*

Isle of Man

Population: 70,000   Capital: *Douglas*

Guernsey

Population: 59,000   Capital: *St. Peter Port*

Jersey

Population: 84,000   Capital: *St. Helier*

Guernsey, the Channel Islands

United States of America

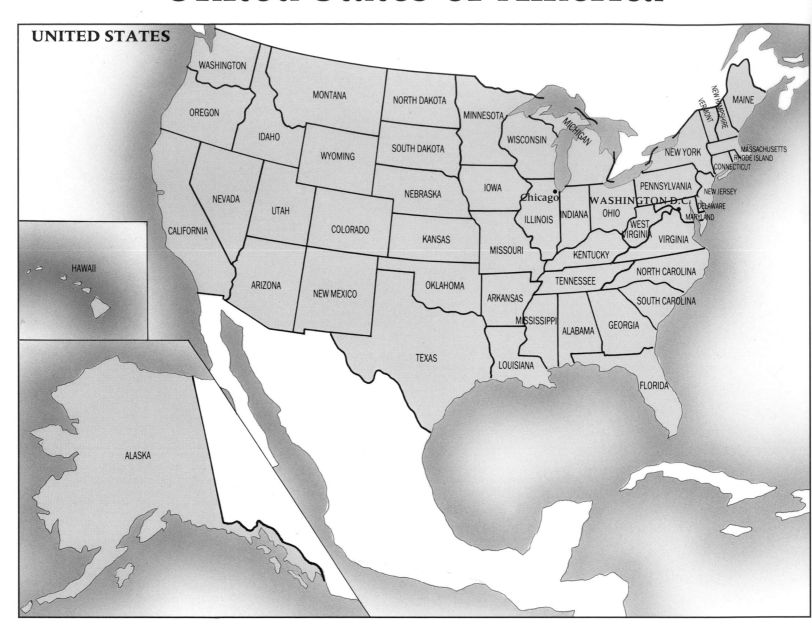

UNITED STATES

Alabama

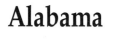

Population: 4,187,000   Capital: *Montgomery*

Alaska

Population: 599,000   Capital: *Juneau*

Arizona

Population: 3,936,000   Capital: *Phoenix*

Arkansas

Population: 2,424,000   Capital: *Little Rock*

California

Population: 31,211,000   Capital: *Sacramento*

Colorado

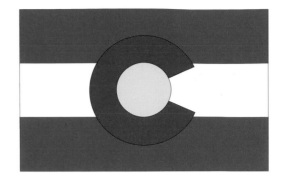

Population: 3,566,000   Capital: *Denver*

Connecticut

Population: 3,277,000   Capital: *Hartford*

Delaware

Population: 700,000   Capital: *Dover*

Florida

Population: 13,679,000   Capital: *Tallahassee*

San Francisco, California

A typical beach scene, Hawaii

Georgia

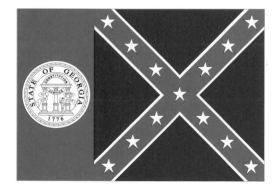

Population: 6,917,000   Capital: *Atlanta*

Hawaii

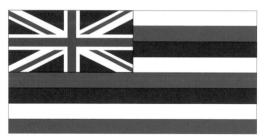

Population: 1,172,000   Capital: *Honolulu*

Idaho

Population: 1,099,000   Capital: *Boise*

Illinois

Population: 11,697,000   Capital: *Springfield*

Indiana

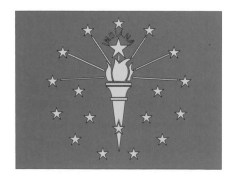

Population: 5,713,000   Capital: *Indianapolis*

Iowa

Population: 2,814,000   Capital: *Des Moines*

Kansas

Population: 2,531,000   **Capital:** *Topeka*

Kentucky

Population: 3,789,000   **Capital:** *Frankfort*

Louisiana

Population: 4,295,000   **Capital:** *Baton Rouge*

Maine

Population: 1,239,000   **Capital:** *Augusta*

Maryland

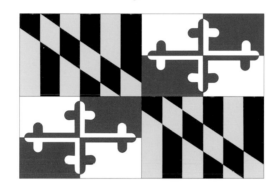

Population: 4,965,000   **Capital:** *Annapolis*

Massachusetts

Population: 6,012,000   **Capital:** *Boston*

The coast of Maine in winter

Michigan

Population: 9,478,000   Capital: *Lansing*

Minnesota

Population: 4,517,000   Capital: *St. Paul*

Mississippi

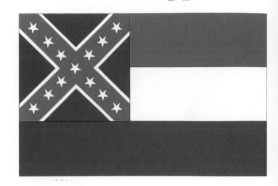

Population: 2,643,000   Capital: *Jackson*

Missouri

Population: 5,234,000   Capital: *Jefferson City*

Montana

Population: 839,000   Capital: *Helena*

Nebraska

Population: 1,607,000   Capital: *Lincoln*

Nevada

Population: 1,389,000   Capital: *Carson City*

New Hampshire

Population: 1,125,000   Capital: *Concord*

New Jersey

Population: 7,879,000   Capital: *Trenton*

New Mexico

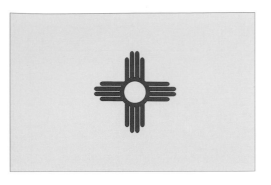

Population: *1,616,000*   Capital: *Santa Fé*

New York

Population: *18,197,000*   Capital: *Albany*

North Carolina

Population: *6,945,000*   Capital: *Raleigh*

North Dakota

Population: *635,000*   Capital: *Bismarck*

Ohio

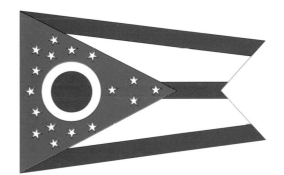

Population: *11,091,000*   Capital: *Columbus*

Oklahoma

Population: *3,231,000*   Capital: *Oklahoma City*

Oregon

Population: *3,032,000*   Capital: *Salem*

Pennsylvania

Population: *12,048,000*   Capital: Harrisburg

Rhode Island

Population: *1,000,000*   Capital: *Providence*

South Carolina

Population: *3,643,000*   Capital: *Columbia*

South Dakota

Population: *715,000*   Capital: *Pierre*

Tennessee

Population: *5,099,000*   Capital: *Nashville*

Turret Arch, Arches National Park, Utah

Texas

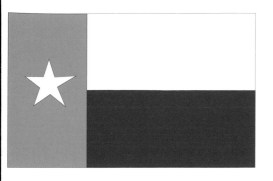

Population: *18,031,000*   Capital: *Austin*

Utah

Population: *1,860,000*   Capital: *Salt Lake City*

Vermont

Population: *576,000*   Capital: *Montpelier*

Turret Arch, National Park, Utah

Virginia

Population: *6,490,000*   Capital: *Richmond*

Washington

Population: *5,255,000*   Capital: *Olympia*

West Virginia

Population: *1,820,000*   Capital: *Charleston*

Wisconsin

Population: *5,038,000*   Capital: *Madison*

Wyoming

Population: *470, 000*   Capital: *Cheyenne*

District of Columbia

Population: *578,000*   Capital: *Washington*

Presidential Flag

Vice-Presidential Flag

The United Nations flag blowing in the wind

International Organizations

Arab League

Commonwealth

European Union

Olympic Games

NATO

United Nations

South-East Asia Organization Treaty

Organization of American States

Organization of African Union

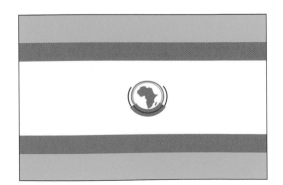

International Red Cross

Red Crescent